CAMPBELL'S
2001 QUIZ QUESTIONS

By John P. Campbell

Campbell's High School/College Quiz Book (Revised Edition)

Campbell's Potpourri I of Quiz Bowl Questions

Campbell's Potpourri II of Quiz Bowl Questions (Revised Edition)

Campbell's Middle School Quiz Book #1

Campbell's Potpourri III of Quiz Bowl Questions

Campbell's Middle School Quiz Book #2

Campbell's Elementary School Quiz Book #1

Campbell's 2001 Quiz Questions

Campbell's Potpourri IV of Quiz Bowl Questions

Campbell's Middle School Quiz Book #3

The 500 Famous Quotations Quiz Book

Campbell's 2002 Quiz Questions

Campbell's 210 Lightning Rounds

CAMPBELL'S 2001 QUIZ QUESTIONS

by John P. Campbell

PATRICK'S PRESS
Columbus, Georgia

Printed in the United States of America

CIP data suggested by the author

Campbell, John P., 1942-
Campbell's 2001 Quiz Questions

Includes index.
Summary: Questions and answers on a wide-range of topics, such as history, literature, geography, sports, the Bible, science, art, mythology, and religion, are arranged into twenty "packets."
1. Questions and answers. [1. Questions and answers]
I. Title II. Title: Campbell's 2001 Quiz Questions.
III. Title: 2001 Quiz Questions
IV. Title: Two Thousand and One Quiz Questions
AG195.C293   1990   031'.02

ISBN (International Standard Book Number): 0-944322-01-8
Library of Congress Catalog Card Numbers
are no longer issued for quiz books

First Edition
First Printing, February 1990; Second Printing, February 1992

ACKNOWLEDGMENTS

I am once again very indebted to Rinda Brewbaker, part-time English teacher at Pacelli High School, for her editing ability and suggestions.

I appreciate the help of Pam Barton, Beth Burdeshaw, Karen Bushaw, Rebecca Cartee, Ben Lewis, Trip Meine, Jennifer Pavlick, and Tippi Faucette for their work in checking and proofreading the material. I also thank Rick Thurman of Georgia Southwestern College for his proofreading assistance and Kim Baxley for her work, especially indexing.

I want to thank my mother, Mrs. John Campbell, for her support.

I thank the following for reading the material, for making corrections and suggestions, and possibly for contributing questions: *American Literature*: Jack Norton, Georgia Southwestern College; *Ancient* and *European History*: Richard L. Baringer, Georgia Southwestern College; *Biology*: Dr. Jack Carter, Georgia Southwestern College; *Chemistry*: Dr. Wayne Counts, Georgia Southwestern College; *English Grammar*: Rinda Brewbaker; *English* and *World Literature*: Dr. Allen D. Towery, Georgia Southwestern College; *Mathematics*: Dr. Jay Cliett; Pamela Coffield, Brookstone School; and Patricia Culpepper, Rothschild Junior High School; *Political Science*: Dr. William L. Chappell, Jr., Columbus College; and Kent M. Sole, Georgia Southwestern College; *U.S. History*: Dr. Frank M. Lowrey, Georgia Southwestern College

I would also like to thank Cornerstone Images of Columbus for their typesetting services.

To

Students in quick recall quiz events whose speed and scope of knowledge are remarkable to begin with and whose capabilities may be enhanced with these 2001 questions.

PREFACE

This book is intended as quiz bowl material not only for the coach of an Academic Bowl team to use in conducting practices but also for individual team members to use as study material. The complete index complements this intention as the users of this book are able to find quickly material they wish to review.

Quiz competitions vary in nature, some with all TOSS-UP questions and some with a TOSS-UP question followed by a BONUS question. This book, unlike my others, follows the all TOSS-UP format.

Your suggestions and comments will be appreciated. Please send them to me care of PATRICK'S PRESS, Box 5189, Columbus, Georgia, 31906.

John Campbell

CONTENTS

CHAPTER ONE

1) Give the English meaning of the Russian word *glasnost*.
   Answer: Openness (forthrightness in publicizing problems and weaknesses of Soviet society).

2) Which type of year is called a *bissextile* year?
   Answer: A leap year (a year denoting the extra day, February 29).

3) Which conflict is known as the "War of Iniquity," the "Unnecessary War," and "Mr. Madison's War"?
   Answer: War of 1812.

4) Give the names of the 2 ships involved in a confrontation off the coast of Virginia on June 22, 1807, in an action that ultimately led to the War of 1812. The British ship fired on the American ship, killing 3, and then dragged 4 "deserters" away.
   Answer: *Leopard* (British) and *Chesapeake* (American).

5) Which word from the Greek for "opposite foot" is used to describe "two places that are exactly opposite each other on the globe"?
   Answer: Antipodes.

6) In British usage, which 2 countries are considered the Antipodes? The English first used the term because these countries are located almost opposite England.
   Answer: Australia and New Zealand.

7) What percentage is the equivalent of 2/5?
   Answer: 40%.

8) If a cricket chirps 120 times a minute, how many times does it chirp in 10 seconds?
   Answer: 20.

9) Give the meaning of the initialism ATV. In 1988, the Justice Department banned the sale of adult-sized ATVs to children

under 16 because of the many deaths they have caused.
Answer: All-Terrain Vehicles.

10) Which all-time leading scorer for which college basketball team
died of a heart attack in 1988? He was known as "Pistol Pete."
Answer: Pete Maravich for Louisiana State University.

11) Identify the product, one of the world's most useful, made chiefly
from inexpensive raw materials such as sand, soda or potash,
and lime or lead oxide.
Answer: Glass.

12) Which term designates the "process that makes glass or metals
less brittle by heating and then cooling them"? This process
removes the stresses and strains left in the glass after shaping.
Answer: Annealing.

13) Which mischievous spirit or elf in English folklore is also called
Robin Goodfellow?
Answer: Puck.

14) Identify the high-spirited niece of Leonato in Shakespeare's
Much Ado About Nothing. She has the same name as the beloved
of Dante.
Answer: Beatrice.

15) In which 1966 case did the U.S. Supreme Court limit the power
of police to question suspects?
Answer: Miranda case (*Miranda v Arizona*).

16) The Supreme Court based its *Miranda* decision on 2 amendments to the U.S. Constitution. Identify both the one which
protects persons from testifying against themselves and the one
which guarantees a defendant's right to a lawyer.
Answer: 5th and 6th, respectively.

17) Who founded the Mormon Church in New York on April 6, 1830?
Answer: Joseph Smith.

18) Who became the Mormon leader after a mob attacked and killed
Joseph Smith on June 27, 1844?
Answer: Brigham Young.

19) In which 2 centuries did the Hundred Years' War take place?
Answer: 14th and 15th (1337-1453).

20) In which battle in 1346, the first great battle of the Hundred Years' War, did English archers and infantry carry the day?
Answer: Crécy.

21) Aboard which space shuttle did 7 U.S. astronauts die on January 28, 1986, in an explosion?
Answer: *Challenger*.

22) Aboard which spacecraft did U.S. Astronauts Virgil Grissom, Edward White, and Roger Chaffee die in 1967 in a flash fire?
Answer: *Apollo*.

23) In which country in a schoolhouse in Reims did the German military leaders surrender to Dwight Eisenhower on May 7, 1945?
Answer: France.

24) Name the plane and the pilot in the May 1960 incident that caused Premier Khrushchev to cancel the 4-Power Summit Conference in Paris.
Answer: U-2 was flown by Francis Gary Powers.

25) Which continent did Roman scholars call *Terra Australis Incognita*, a Latin term for *Unknown Southern Land*? Tribes in New Zealand referred to it as the great white land to the south.
Answer: Antarctica (accept Australia as Roman scholars also once called it *Terra Australis Incognita*).

26) Who were Australia's first settlers? This group of people, whose name is derived from the Latin for "from the beginning," reached this continent 40-50,000 years ago.
Answer: Aborigines.

27) In what number base are the calculations of a computer's central processing unit (CPU) done?
Answer: 2 (binary).

28) To which one of the following types of data structures does a linked list belong: static, variable, or dynamic?
Answer: Dynamic.

29) Which leader of which country exceeded 8 years and 244 days in office to become the country's longest continuously serving prime minister of the 20th century when she was reelected in December 1987?
Answer: Margaret Thatcher of Great Britain.

30) In which country did Communist rebels under Enver Hoxha seize power in 1944? The capital of this country, which Hoxha ruled until his death in 1985, is Tirana.
Answer: Albania.

31) Give the word for a structure of wax containing rows of 6-sided cells made by bees to store their honey.
Answer: Honeycomb.

32) What is the meaning of the word *Deseret* in the Book of Mormon? The Mormons adopted this type of insect as its symbol of hard work.
Answer: Honeybee (Land of the Honeybee).

33) Identify the Persian royal astronomer whose epithet meaning "The Tentmaker" is probably derived from his father's trade.
Answer: Omar Khayyám.

34) In 1859, which Englishman translated the quatrains of the *Rubáiyát of Omar Khayyám*?
Answer: Edward FitzGerald.

35) Which type of machine is called a polygraph?
Answer: Lie detector.

36) Which country's dignified national dance is called the *Polonaise*.
Answer: Poland's.

37) How many months did Romulus, the alleged creator, include in the 1st Roman calendar?
Answer: 10.

38) Which Roman leader moved the beginning of the year from March to January, making February the 2nd month?
Answer: Julius Caesar (accept Numa Pubilius, according to another source).

39) In which West German city was Spandau Prison before it was torn down so it would not become a Nazi shrine?
Answer: West Berlin.

40) Who was the last person incarcerated in Spandau Prison? He was Hitler's secretary, who was sentenced to life imprisonment in 1946 for war crimes.
Answer: Rudolf Hess.

41) What is the positive square root of the product of 3, 6, and 2?
Answer: 6.

42) If bananas are 98 cents a pound, how much is a bunch of bananas weighing 8 ounces?
Answer: 49 cents.

43) Name the greatest battle of the War of 1812, known as the "Unnecessary" or "Needless Battle," which was fought 15 days after the peace treaty had been signed.
Answer: Battle of New Orleans.

44) Although the Battle of New Orleans was fought on January 8, 1815, in which city in which country had the peace treaty been signed on December 24, 1814, ending the War of 1812?
Answer: Ghent, Belgium (known as the Treaty of Ghent).

45) Which inland sea or lake in North America is fed by freshwater streams yet is saltier than the oceans? This body of water is the largest salt water lake in North America.
Answer: Great Salt Lake.

46) Identify the largest lake in the Southern United States. Its name is derived from a Seminole Indian word that means "plenty big water."
Answer: Lake Okeechobee.

47) What is the sine of 1.5 pi radians?
Answer: Negative 1.

48) In the radian system of measuring angles, how many radians is one-fourth revolution or 90 degrees?
Answer: pi/2 radians.

49) What is the official residence of the prime minister of Great Britain?
Answer: 10 Downing Street.

50) Name the British prime minister whose term of office from 1908 to 1916 was surpassed by that of Margaret Thatcher.
Answer: Herbert Henry Asquith.

51) Identify the birds that are both the tallest and among the rarest birds in North America. These symbols of wildlife conservation are also called "whoopers" because of their loud, buglelike call.
Answer: Whooping cranes.

52) The name *whooping cough* is derived from the high-pitched, whooping noise victims make when trying to catch their breath after coughing attacks. What is the medical term for *whooping cough*?
Answer: Pertussis.

53) Identify the youngest of the 3 great Greek tragedians, less successful than the other two, and the author of *Orestes* and *The Bacchae*.
Answer: Euripides.

54) Identify the tragedy by Euripides in which the central character gets revenge on Jason.
Answer: *Medea*.

55) Which phrase means "an unexpected winner; an obscure person in politics who gets the nomination for office unexpectedly, usually by a compromise after a deadlock in the selection process"?
Answer: Dark horse.

56) Name the 11th U.S. President, the first one to fit the description of a dark-horse candidate.
Answer: James K. Polk.

57) Who is the patron saint of hopeless causes?
Answer: St. Jude.

58) Which evangelist in which Oklahoma city said in 1987 that he needed to raise $8 million for his World Outreach Program to prevent God from taking his life?
Answer: Oral Roberts in Tulsa.

59) Identify the hill that was the site of Roman emperor Nero's public gardens and circus, and where, according to tradition, the first pope, St. Peter, was crucified.
Answer: Vatican Hill.

60) In which city in which country did the popes of the Roman Catholic Church live from 1309 to 1377?
Answer: Avignon, France.

61) Which relatively new word, derived from 2 Greek words, literally means "against life"? This word designates a drug that may save human lives by acting to end the life of germs.
Answer: Antibiotic.

62) After a successful inoculation campaign in Asia, which organization, known as WHO, announced in 1979 that smallpox had been wiped out?
Answer: World Health Organization.

63) During which U.S. President's administration did the Teapot Dome scandal occur?
Answer: Warren Harding's.

64) Identify the Secretary of the Interior of the Harding administration who became the first Cabinet member ever jailed as a criminal.
Answer: Albert Fall.

65) The official language of all Central American countries is Spanish except for which one country?
Answer: Belize.

66) Give the former name of Belize.
Answer: British Honduras.

67) Which Greek letter refers to the ratio of a circle's circumference to its diameter?
Answer: Pi.

68) Name the 4 smallest numbers in the set of natural numbers.
Answer: 1, 2, 3, and 4.

69) In which city did the collapse of a new Ashland Oil Company storage tank pour an estimated one million gallons of diesel oil into the Monongahela River in January 1988?
Answer: Pittsburgh.

70) Two rivers meet to form a third river at the Golden Triangle in Pittsburgh. The Monongahela is one of the 3 rivers; name the other 2.
Answer: Ohio and the Allegheny (the Monongahela and the Allegheny meet to form the Ohio).

71) Which 3-word term is used in physics to designate "that point in a body around which its weight is evenly balanced in all positions"?
Answer: Center of gravity (accept center of mass).

72) Which 3-word term is used in physics to designate "a point in a floating body, corresponding to the center of gravity of the water displaced"?
Answer: Center of buoyancy.

73) Identify the New York-born brother of Henry James who led a philosophical movement called pragmatism.
Answer: William James.

74) Which author from which country wrote *Cry, the Beloved Country*?
Answer: Alan Paton from South Africa.

75) Which agency was created by Congress in 1865 to fight the counterfeiting of U.S. currency?
Answer: Secret Service.

76) The Secret Service began protecting the U.S. President in 1901 after the assassination of which President?
Answer: William McKinley.

77) Which word based on the Bible's Book of Revelation (20: 1-6) means "the period of a thousand years during which Christ will

reign on earth." In general the word means "a period of happiness, righteousness, and peace; an imagined golden age."
Answer: Millennium.

78) Which Biblical monster defeated by God has the same name as a treatise by Thomas Hobbes?
Answer: Leviathan.

79) Identify the African country settled by freed American slaves in 1822.
Answer: Liberia.

80) Identify the U.S. President after whom the capital of Liberia is named.
Answer: James Monroe (Monrovia is the capital).

81) Which Revolutionary War general became America's most infamous traitor with his plan to betray West Point to the British?
Answer: Benedict Arnold.

82) Which U.S. Army private was shot to death for desertion by a firing squad on January 31, 1945?
Answer: Private Eddie Slovik.

83) In which New York city was President McKinley assassinated at the Pan American Exposition in 1901?
Answer: Buffalo.

84) Who assassinated President McKinley in 1901?
Answer: Leon F. Czolgosz.

85) Identify the U.S. capital the French once called *la Petite Roche*.
Answer: Little Rock (Arkansas).

86) Which 2 states bordering Arkansas are separated from it by the Mississippi River?
Answer: Tennessee and Mississippi.

87) Name the author of *The Elements*, a book on elementary geometry used as a textbook for about 2,000 years. He is known as "The Father of Geometry."
Answer: Euclid.

88) In geometry, what kind of statement must be proven before it is accepted?
Answer: Theorem.

89) After the assassination of which Democratic presidential candidate in 1968 did the Secret Service begin protecting candidates?
Answer: Robert Kennedy.

90) In which city was W. Wilson Goode elected as the city's first black mayor in 1983?
Answer: Philadelphia.

91) Identify the bone disease that occurs mostly in children under 3 years of age. This disease results in conditions called bowlegs, knockknees, and rosary ribs.
Answer: Rickets.

92) Which disease caused by *rickettsias* may have killed more than 3,000,000 people in Russia and Eastern Poland during the revolutionary period that followed WWI?
Answer: Typhus.

93) Identify the American poet who recited his poem "The Gift Outright" at John F. Kennedy's inauguration on January 20, 1961.
Answer: Robert Frost.

94) Is the author of what is generally considered to be the first American novel, *The Power of Sympathy, or the Triumph of Nature*, published in 1789, Charles Brockden Brown, William Hill Brown, Washington Irving, or James Fenimore Cooper?
Answer: William Hill Brown.

95) How many strings does a violin have?
Answer: 4.

96) What is the term used to describe the plucking of the violin strings with the fingers?
Answer: Pizzicato.

97) Which literary form named from the Greek for "goat song" grew out of the celebrations in honor of the Greek god Dionysus?
Answer: Tragedy.

98) Whose use of the term *Oedipus complex* to describe certain features of infantile sexuality led to numerous translations and adaptations of the Theban plays of Sophocles?
Answer: Sigmund Freud's.

99) In 1948, all the Central American countries except Belize joined with other Latin American countries and the U.S. to form the OAS. Identify the OAS.
Answer: Organization of American States.

100) Identify the 2 Indian groups of Mexico and Central America that developed advanced civilizations that included written languages and large cities.
Answer: Aztecs and Mayas.

CHAPTER TWO

1) How many times does the equator cross the International Date Line?
   Answer: Once.

2) Identify the 2 symbols of the 12 signs of the Zodiac that are invertebrates.
   Answer: Crab and scorpion.

3) The British government formerly claimed the right to stop neutral ships on the high seas and the right to remove sailors of British birth. Give the term for this policy of forcing men into naval service.
   Answer: Impressment.

4) Which French minister to the U.S. in 1793 so outraged American sensibilities when he began to arm ships in American ports that President Washington demanded his recall?
   Answer: Edmond "Citizen" Genet.

5) Within 1000 miles, what is the circumference of the earth at the equator?
   Answer: 25,000 miles (accept 24,000 to 26,000 miles).

6) Which 2 continents are completely below or south of the equator?
   Answer: Australia and Antarctica.

7) In simplest form, what is the ratio of surface area to volume for a cube that measures 4 cm on each side?
   Answer: 3 to 2.

8) Find the volume of a right circular cone with a base of 2 and a height of 6.
   Answer: 4.

9) Give the meaning of the acronym START, the label given to the talks between the Soviet Union and the U.S.
Answer: Strategic Arms Reduction Talks.

10) In Mikhail Gorbachev's fight to radically restructure the Soviet Union, which Russian word designates his economic and political restructuring?
Answer: *Perestroika.*

11) Is a whale more closely related to a fish, a shark, a dog, or a sponge?
Answer: Dog.

12) Give another name for hydrocyanic acid, so called because it was first obtained from a dark blue solid substance with a coppery luster.
Answer: Prussic acid.

13) What poetic term designates unrhymed verse written in iambic pentameter?
Answer: Blank verse.

14) Which character in which Shakespearean play who enjoys playing pranks on human beings says, "Lord, what fools these mortals be!"?
Answer: Puck in *A Midsummer Night's Dream.*

15) Identify the first President for whom 18-year-olds in the U.S. were able to vote.
Answer: Richard Nixon.

16) Which amendment adopted in which year gave 18-year-olds the right to vote?
Answer: 26th Amendment in 1971.

17) Which king of Israel has more chapters of the Bible devoted to his reign than any other monarch?
Answer: David.

18) Who was King Saul's son with whom David, the 2nd king of Israel, formed a close relationship?
Answer: Jonathan.

19) Which West German chancellor, who took office in 1969 and resigned in 1974, began a drive to normalize relations with the Communist bloc?
Answer: Willy Brandt.

20) What is the German word for "Opening to the East," a drive started by West German Chancellor Willy Brandt to normalize relations with the Communist bloc, including East Germany?
Answer: *Ostpolitik.*

21) Which U.S. city was once called the Federal City?
Answer: Washington, D.C.

22) On which U.S. coin and which bill do George Washington's portraits appear?
Answer: Quarter and the $1 bill.

23) Which "Boy Orator of the Platte" roused the 1896 Democratic convention with a speech about not pressing down upon the brow of labor a crown of thorns nor crucifying mankind on a cross of gold?
Answer: William Jennings Bryan.

24) Identify the second Secretary of State in the Washington administration who the President believed might have sold secrets to the French.
Answer: Edmund Randolph.

25) Which Eastern U.S. city is known as the "City of Brotherly Love"?
Answer: Philadelphia (Pennsylvania).

26) Which Eastern U.S. city is nicknamed "Beantown"?
Answer: Boston (Massachusetts).

27) Of the Witch of Agnesi, the Folium of Descartes, and the Rhind Papyrus, which one is a mathematical document?
Answer: Rhind Papyrus.

28) Give the formula of Swiss mathematician Leonhard Euler which relates the number of vertices (v), faces (f), and edges (e) of a polyhedra.
Answer: Vertices plus faces = edges plus two ($v + f = e + 2$).

29) Identify the leader of the Polish Solidarity movement whose *A Way of Hope: An Autobiography* was published in 1988.
Answer: Lech Walesa.

30) Give the meaning of AARP, the U.S. group with 27 million members, which has emerged as the nation's most powerful special-interest lobby.
Answer: American Association for Retired Persons.

31) What is the more common name for anaerobic respiration or anaerobic glycolysis, the process by which living cells degrade sugar?
Answer: Fermentation.

32) During the process of fermentation, yeast breaks down sugar obtained from malted grain into ethyl alcohol and which other gas for use in beer?
Answer: Carbon dioxide.

33) Identify the English poet who was sometimes called the "Swan of the River Avon."
Answer: William Shakespeare.

34) Which Shakespearean play is named after a storm at sea?
Answer: *The Tempest.*

35) Which U.S. President-to-be organized a relief program that fed 10 million civilians in German-occupied Belgium after Britain blockaded the coast during World War I?
Answer: Herbert Hoover.

36) Which artist's U.S. Capitol rotunda fresco containing 13 maidens, supposedly representing the first 13 states, underwent a $500,000 restoration in 1988? George Washington is the subject of this fresco.
Answer: Constantine Brumidi's.

37) Vanna White became famous as the hostess of TV's *Wheel of Fortune*, but which goddess in Roman mythology, identified with the Greek Tyche, was often depicted with the wheel of fortune in medieval art and literature?
Answer: Fortuna (normally depicted today with a rudder and cornucopia).

38) Give the mythological name of the group of Alecto (the unresting), Tisiphone (the jealous), and Megaera (the avenger). These were the terrible goddesses of vengeance in Greek and Roman mythology.
Answer: The Furies (or Erinyes).

39) What is the European name for the war known in the U.S. as the French and Indian War?
Answer: Seven Years' War.

40) What is the European name for the war known in the U.S. as Queen Anne's War?
Answer: War of Spanish Succession.

41) What is the perimeter of a regular hexagon if one side measures 9.4 meters?
Answer: 56.4 meters.

42) The total surface area of a cube is 150 square centimeters. What is the length of one edge?
Answer: 5 centimeters.

43) The bombardment of which fort in Baltimore, Maryland, in September 1814, inspired Francis Scott Key to write "The Star-Spangled Banner"?
Answer: Fort McHenry.

44) Name the 2 U.S. Presidents who, prior to their election, won military fame during the War of 1812. One defeated the British at the Battle of New Orleans, and the other defeated a combined British and Indian force at the Battle of the Thames.
Answer: Andrew Jackson and William Henry Harrison.

45) Mushrooms differ from green plants because they lack which green substance such plants use to make food?
Answer: Chlorophyll.

46) Which Chicago museum is the oldest and largest contemporary science and technology museum in the U.S.? It opened in 1933.
Answer: Museum of Science and Industry.

47) Goldbach's conjecture is that every even number except 2 is equal to the sum of how many prime numbers?
Answer: 2.

48) Goldbach's conjecture states that every number greater than 4
is the sum of 2 odd primes. What are the 2 odd primes of the
number 12?
Answer: 5 and 7.

49) For which new Cabinet post did President Bush swear in
Edward J. Derwinski in 1989?
Answer: Department of Veterans Affairs.

50) Name the Pulitzer Prize-winning cartoonist of the *Chicago Sun-
Times* and creator of the bedraggled WWII characters Willie and
Joe. He was present when Edward J. Derwinski was sworn in as
the secretary of Veterans Affairs.
Answer: Bill Mauldin.

51) Which English chemist formulated the law of partial pressures
in gases in 1802?
Answer: John Dalton.

52) Identify the series of chemical reactions, also known as the citric
acid cycle or the tricarboxylic acid cycle, that take place in all
cells that require oxygen to live. This cycle is named after the
German biochemist who shared the 1953 Nobel Prize in physiology or medicine for discovering the process.
Answer: Krebs cycle.

53) In literature, who is Henry Fielding's foundling?
Answer: Tom Jones.

54) Identify the evil hypnotist in George du Maurier's novel *Trilby*.
This character's name today refers to "a person who completely
dominates another, usually with selfish motives."
Answer: Svengali.

55) What is the meaning of the word *stentorian*? This word is derived from the Greek herald in the Trojan War, who is described
as having a certain type of voice.
Answer: "very loud" (as having the voice of 50 men).

56) Identify the Trojan prince whose name today is used both as a
noun meaning "a bully" and as a verb meaning "to intimidate."
He was killed by Achilles.
Answer: Hector.

57) Who said in 1964, "The medium is the message"?
Answer: Marshall H. McLuhan.

58) Give the name for the cloth in which, according to religious tradition, the body of Jesus Christ was wrapped in his tomb.
Answer: Shroud of Turin.

59) Who was queen of England from 1558 until her death in 1603?
Answer: Elizabeth I.

60) Which Protestant denomination did Elizabeth I make her country's main church?
Answer: Church of England (accept Anglican Church).

61) Which animal's name is used to name the center of a dart board?
Answer: Bull's (eye).

62) Identify the only wild monkey now living in Europe, one that lives on the British dependency of Gibraltar.
Answer: Barbary Ape.

63) Which WWII American general died of injuries suffered in an automobile accident in December 1945 and was buried in the Third Army cemetery in Luxembourg?
Answer: General George S. Patton.

64) More of this state's governors have become Presidents of the U.S. than any other. Name it.
Answer: New York.

65) In which state was gold discovered by carpenter John Marshall while he was building a sawmill on January 24, 1848?
Answer: California.

66) At whose sawmill in which valley did John Marshall discover gold?
Answer: (John) Sutter's mill in Sacramento Valley.

67) Multiply 3 squared times negative 1.
Answer: Negative 9.

68) Give the formula for finding the area of a circle.
Answer: Area = πr^2 (pi r squared).

69) From which country, where tribesmen called themselves "mujahedeen" (mujahedin) or "holy warriors," did the Soviet Union begin to withdraw its troops in May 1988?
Answer: Afghanistan.

70) Give the day, the month, and the date in 1987 when the stock market suffered its worst loss ever when it fell 508 points.
Answer: (Bloody or Black) Monday, October 19.

71) What name is given to the biological concept that living things come from nonliving things?
Answer: Spontaneous generation, or abiogenesis, or autogenesis.

72) What are the 3 products of the complete digestion of carbohydrates, fats, and proteins?
Answer: Simple sugars (glucose), fatty acids (and glycerol), and amino acids.

73) Which French playwright was born Jean Baptiste Poquelin?
Answer: Molière.

74) What is the English title of the play *Le Malade Imaginaire* in which Molière was performing when he died?
Answer: *The Imaginary Invalid.*

75) Which Peruvian became the secretary-general of the U.N. in 1982?
Answer: Javier Pérez de Cuéllar.

76) Name 3 of the 5 permanent members of the U.N. Security Council.
Answer: United States, Soviet Union, Great Britain, France, and People's Republic of China.

77) Who was born Karol Wojtyla in Poland in 1920?
Answer: Pope John Paul II.

78) Give the name for the Pope's own Vatican guards who accompany him on trips.
Answer: Swiss Guards.

79) What name is given to the French Republic of which Charles de Gaulle was the president from 1959 to 1969?
Answer: Fifth Republic.

80) With which African country did Charles de Gaulle reach an agreement leading to this country's independent status in 1962?
Answer: Algeria.

81) A magazine described the battle over the confirmation of Robert Bork to the U.S. Supreme Court as a donnybrook. Give the meaning of *donnybrook*.
Answer: "A rough fight" or "free-for-all."

82) Senator Biden's anti-Bork stance before the hearings reminded one senator of which character in which work by Lewis Carroll who says, "Sentence first, verdict afterwards"?
Answer: Queen of Hearts in *Alice's Adventures in Wonderland*.

83) Which future U.S. President wrote on January 16, 1787, "Were it left to me to decide whether we should have a government without newspapers, or newspapers without a government, I should not hesitate a moment to prefer the latter"?
Answer: Thomas Jefferson.

84) Name the first 2 black Americans to win the Nobel Peace Prize.
Answer: Ralph Bunche (1950) and Martin Luther King, Jr. (1964).

85) In which U.S. city, known as the "Windy City," did 28,000 teachers go on strike in 1987?
Answer: Chicago.

86) In which African country is the Serengeti National Park?
Answer: Tanzania.

87) What is the value of 27 raised to the negative 2/3 power?
Answer: 1/9.

88) What is the value of 8 to the 2/3 power?
Answer: 4.

89) Give the name for "a citizen of the Soviet Union who is refused permission by the authorities to leave the country."
Answer: Refusnik (or refusenik).

90) Give the Russian word for "a system by which manuscripts denied official publication in the Soviet Union are circulated secretly in mimeograph form, or smuggled out for publication abroad."
Answer: *Samizdat.*

91) A fruit fly has a diploid number of 8 chromosomes. How many chromosomes does the sperm cell of a male fruit fly contain?
Answer: 4.

92) The half-life of Carbon-14 is 5730 years. How old is a fossil containing 1/8 of the original Carbon-14?
Answer: 17,190 years.

93) Identify the Missouri-born author of *The Waste Land* and winner of the 1948 Nobel Prize for literature.
Answer: T.S. Eliot.

94) In which work by which author did Phileas Fogg say on October 2, 1872, "I will bet 20,000 pounds with anyone, that I shall make the tour of the world in eighty days or less"?
Answer: *Around the World in Eighty Days* by Jules Verne.

95) Identify the former governor of Kansas who celebrated his 100th birthday in 1987. He was the Republican candidate for President in 1936.
Answer: Alf Landon.

96) Identify the only 2 states Alf Landon carried in the 1936 presidential election for a total of 8 electoral votes.
Answer: Maine and Vermont.

97) Pope John Paul is considered to be the most peripatetic of Roman Catholic pontiffs. Give the meaning of *peripatetic*.
Answer: "Moving from place to place."

98) Give the word used by Roman Catholics to describe the Pope as being incapable of error when he makes formal pronouncements on doctrines of faith and morals.
Answer: Infallible.

99) Which king of France who reigned from 1643-1715 was known as the "Sun King"?
Answer: Louis XIV.

100) Which cardinal acting as chief minister dominated the early part of the reign of Louis XIV?
Answer: Cardinal Mazarin.

CHAPTER THREE

1) Give the word for "the state or practice of having 2 or more wives or husbands at the same time."
   Answer: Polygamy.

2) On which person's grave in which city is the epitaph, "Free at last, free at last, thank God Almighty, I'm free at last"?
   Answer: Martin Luther King, Jr. in Atlanta (Georgia).

3) Which massacre occurred in Chicago on February 14, 1929, when members of the Bugsy Moran gang were lined up and shot?
   Answer: St. Valentine's Day Massacre.

4) Name the Maryland-born spokesman of American blacks who founded the *North Star*, an antislavery newspaper.
   Answer: Frederick Douglass.

5) *Taiwan* is the Chinese name meaning "terraced bay." Give the Portuguese name for this mountainous island country meaning "beautiful island."
   Answer: (Ilha) Formosa.

6) Name the longest river of South Africa. This river has the same name as a secondary color.
   Answer: Orange River.

7) The cosine of what acute angle is equal to the sine of 20 degrees?
   Answer: 70.

8) In the radian system of measuring angles, how many radians is one-sixth revolution or 60 degrees?
   Answer: Pi/3 radians.

9) For which college team did Heisman Trophy winner Doug Flutie play?
   Answer: Boston College.

10) For which 2 teams did Bo Jackson play professionally from 1987-1990?
Answer: Kansas City Royals (began playing for the Chicago White Sox in 1991) and Los Angeles Raiders.

11) According to which theory in biology do living things descend only from living things?
Answer: Biogenesis.

12) Identify the English biologist with the first names of Thomas Henry who coined the word *Biogenesis* in 1870.
Answer: Thomas Henry Huxley.

13) Which American poet wrote, "I think that I shall never see / A poem lovely as a tree"?
Answer: Joyce Kilmer.

14) What did A.E. Housman call the "loveliest of trees"?
Answer: Cherry tree.

15) Which instrument of the violin family is held between the knees in an upright position?
Answer: Cello (or violoncello).

16) Considered the greatest cellist in the 20th century, he was born in Spain in 1876 and went into voluntary exile in France in 1939 to protest Franco's overthrow of the Spanish republic. Name him.
Answer: Pablo Casals.

17) Which country in 1988 marked the millennium of Prince Vladimir's choice of Christianity as the faith of his people?
Answer: Soviet Union.

18) Identify the structure in Jerusalem built over the rock from which, according to Muslim belief, Muhammad rose to heaven with the angel Gabriel.
Answer: Dome of the Rock.

19) Which country celebrated its bicentennial in January 1988, the anniversary of the arrival of the first shipload of convicts from Britain at New South Wales?
Answer: Australia.

20) Give the French phrase for the French nuclear striking force.
Answer: *Force de frappe.*

21) Identify the Italian artist who drew plans for a flying machine and a parachute in the 16th century.
Answer: **Leonardo da Vinci.**

22) What name is given to the giant atom smasher awarded to Texas that was projected to cost $4.4 billion to build?
Answer: **Supercollider.**

23) Who was the first U.S. Vice President who did not become President?
Answer: **Aaron Burr.**

24) By September 1789, the U.S. Congress had established 3 of the departments that make up the cabinet. An Attorney General was added later. Name 2 of these first 3 Cabinet offices.
Answer: **State, War, and Treasury.**

25) Identify the Chinese city whose name in lower case means "to obtain a person, especially a sailor, for the crew of a ship by force."
Answer: **Shanghai.**

26) Which river in China is sometimes called "China's Sorrow" because it frequently floods, bringing death and hunger to those living along its banks?
Answer: **Yellow River (or Hwang Ho).**

27) What is the sum of the infinite geometric series 9/10 + 9/100 + 9/1000?
Answer: **1.**

28) What is the sum of the odd integers between 6 and 18?
Answer: **72.**

29) Identify the country of General Mohammed Zia, accused by the U.S. State Department in 1988 of being involved in a plot to smuggle materials for nuclear devices out of the U.S. Zia was killed in a plane crash later in the year.
Answer: **Pakistan.**

30) Name the Costa Rican President who won the 1987 Nobel Peace
Prize.
Answer: Oscar Arias.

31) Identify the "Father of the Soviet Hydrogen Bomb," who was
freed from internal exile in early 1987.
Answer: Andrei Sakharov.

32) Identify the "Father of the American Hydrogen Bomb," who was
engaged to work on the Star Wars program of President Reagan.
Answer: Edward Teller.

33) Which character created by John D. MacDonald first appeared
in *The Deep Blue Good-Bye* and later in *The Lonely Silver Rain*?
Answer: Travis McGee.

34) In which state does John MacDonald's character Travis McGee
live on his houseboat *The Busted Flush*?
Answer: Florida (Fort Lauderdale).

35) Identify the former U.S. Supreme Court Chief Justice who
became the head of the national Bicentennial Commission.
Answer: Warren E. Burger.

36) Which states did Nancy Kassebaum and Barbara Mikulski
represent as U.S. senators in the late 1980s?
Answer: Kansas (Kassebaum) and Maryland (Mikulski).

37) The Russian word *glasnost*, meaning "openness," is a new word
to Western vocabularies. Which Russian word for an artificial
satellite literally means "co-traveler"?
Answer: *Sputnik*.

38) Give the meaning of the Russian word *apparatchik*.
**Answer: A member, especially an official, of a Commu-
nist Party; a bureaucrat.**

39) Which female world leader was chosen as *Time* magazine's 1986
"Woman of the Year" after she became the leader of an island
country in the southwest Pacific Ocean?
Answer: Corazon Aquino.

40) Name the only 2 other women chosen as *Time* magazine's
"Woman of the Year," one in 1936, the wife of Edward VIII, and

the other in 1952, the Queen of England.
Answer: Wallis Warfield Simpson (Duchess of Windsor) and Queen Elizabeth.

41) What is the common logarithm for 10,000,000?
Answer: 7.

42) What is the x coordinate of the vertex of the parabola whose equation is $y = 3x^2 - 6$ (*y equals three x squared minus six*)?
Answer: 0.

43) Identify the American cartoonist whose cartoon of a jackass wearing a lion's skin frightening away the other animals in the forest helped popularize the donkey as the symbol of the Democratic Party.
Answer: Thomas Nast.

44) Identify the German geographer and map-maker who named America after Amerigo Vespucci.
Answer: Martin Waldseemüller.

45) What was the former name of the African country now called Burkina Faso?
Answer: Upper Volta.

46) Give the 2 official languages of the African country of Cameroon.
Answer: French and English.

47) If the perimeter of a square is represented by $4y$, then which expression represents its area?
Answer: *y* squared.

48) If the length of a rectangle is 2 times its width, what is the width if the perimeter is 24 feet?
Answer: 4 feet.

49) Who was *Time* magazine's 1987 "Man of the Year"? This leader's cover portrait was taken from one on a Russian lacquered box.
Answer: Mikhail Gorbachev.

50) In which U.S. city was Marion Barry, Jr., sworn in to an unprecedented 3rd 4-year term as mayor in 1987?
Answer: Washington, D.C.

51) Which planet, about 25% closer to the sun than the Earth and known as Earth's twin, might have developed like Earth except for its thick atmosphere?
Answer: Venus.

52) Identify the 9th planet and its moon, which together are said by some astronomers to comprise a double planet enveloped in a single atmosphere. The moon is named after a mythological ferryman.
Answer: Pluto and Charon.

53) Which American author wrote *The Call of the Wild*?
Answer: Jack London.

54) Which American author became identified with the ideal of rising from poverty to success through hard work and honesty, as exemplified by the heroes of his popular *Ragged Dick Series*?
Answer: Horatio Alger, Jr.

55) What fraction of the members of the U.S. Senate are up for re-election when elections are held every 2 years?
Answer: 1/3.

56) Under which amendment to the U.S. Constitution does one session of Congress end its term at noon on January 3 and the next Congress begin its term at the same time?
Answer: 20th Amendment.

57) Identify the Austrian known as the "Father of Psychoanalysis."
Answer: Sigmund Freud.

58) Identify the 3 parts into which Freud divided the mind.
Answer: The id, the ego, and the superego.

59) In which Communist bloc country did Erich Honecker become the leader in 1976?
Answer: East Germany.

60) Which Russian leader in which year had the Berlin Wall erected?
Answer: Nikita Khrushchev in 1961.

61) Which botanical term designates a popular plant native to Peru with fragrant flowers always facing toward the sun?
Answer: Heliotrope (accept turnsole).

62) Leaves contain long tubelike structures called *veins*. Which term designates the arrangement of the veins in a leaf blade?
Answer: Venation.

63) With which war is the cry "Remember the Maine" associated?
Answer: Spanish-American War.

64) In which harbor in which year was the American battleship the *Maine* blown up while at anchor on February 15 with the loss of 260 crew members?
Answer: Havana (Cuba) in 1898.

65) Which Georges Bizet opera based on a novelette by Prosper Mérimée was used by both Debi Thomas and Katarina Witt during their climactic skating routines at the 1988 Olympics in Calgary?
Answer: *Carmen.*

66) Scottish sailor Alexander Selkirk was rescued from the uninhabited Juan Fernandez Island on February 1, 1709. His adventures formed the basis of which novel by which English author?
Answer: *Robinson Crusoe* by Daniel Defoe.

67) What is the base of common or Briggs' logarithms?
Answer: Base of 10.

68) When the logarithm of 10 is added to the logarithm of 100, what is the result?
Answer: log 1000 (accept 3).

69) Name the NATO country that after WWII had the world's 3rd largest navy, but now lacks the ships to protect the Northwest Passage, a sea route from the Atlantic through the Arctic to the Pacific.
Answer: Canada.

70) Which country owns the islands of Miquelon and St. Pierre that are located near the Canadian province of Newfoundland?
Answer: France.

71) Which French scientist disproved the theory of spontaneous generation?
Answer: Louis Pasteur.

72) Which theory states that "ontogeny recapitulates phylogeny"?
Answer: Biogenetic, or recapitulation theory.

73) Give the word for the "fear of the number 13."
Answer: Triskaidekaphobia.

74) Give the word for the "fear of Fridays."
Answer: Friggaphobia.

75) Who is the composer of the opera *La Traviata*, which is based on the story of Camille?
Answer: Giuseppe Verdi.

76) What is the name of the 1852 play by Alexandre Dumas from which *Camille* is adapted?
Answer: *La Dame aux camélias.*

77) What is the sign of the Zodiac for January 20 to February 18, the 11th period in the astrological chart?
Answer: Aquarius.

78) Identify the English economist who wrote *Essay on the Principles of Population*. This economist believed that population would increase more rapidly than food supplies.
Answer: Thomas Malthus.

79) According to legend, in which country, known as the "Land of the Rising Sun," did Jimmu Tenno, a descendant of the sun goddess, become the first emperor in 660 B.C.?
Answer: Japan.

80) Which country celebrates its national holiday, Cinco de Mayo, on May 5, the anniversary of the 1862 Battle of Puebla, in which General Zaragoza's troops defeated the French troops of Napoleon III?
Answer: Mexico.

81) Which American said, "Genius is one percent inspiration and ninety-nine percent perspiration"?
Answer: Thomas Edison.

82) Of which city in which state was Thomas Edison known as the "Wizard"?
Answer: ("Wizard of") Menlo Park in New Jersey.

83) Identify the Illinois-born U.S. President whose autobiography is entitled *Where's the Rest of Me?*
Answer: Ronald Reagan.

84) Which Kentucky senator said in a Senate speech on February 1, 1839, "I'd rather be right than be president"?
Answer: Henry Clay.

85) Identify the South American country whose name is derived from the Latin word for silver.
Answer: Argentina (from *argentum*).

86) Which 2 South American countries were named after people, one after a Venezuelan general and the other after an Italian explorer?
Answer: Bolivia and Colombia.

87) Find 2 consecutive integers whose sum is 47.
Answer: 23 and 24.

88) Subtract negative 2 from negative 7.
Answer: Negative 5.

89) Which entertainer is the subject of the autobiography *Moonwalk*?
Answer: Michael Jackson.

90) Identify the 18th-century priest who founded Capistrano and 8 other California missions. Pope John Paul II beatified him in September 1988.
Answer: Father Junípero Serra.

91) To which class do geese and eagles belong?
Answer: Aves.

92) Identify the deciduous tree of China and Japan that is a "living fossil," the only remaining species of a large order of gymnosperms that existed in the Triassic Period.
Answer: Ginkgo (or maidenhair tree).

93) Which English writer used Boz as a pen name?
Answer: Charles Dickens.

94) Which novel by which author is set in the fictional Gopher Prairie, Minnesota, based on the real-life Sauk Centre, Minnesota, where this author was born?
Answer: *Main Street* **by Sinclair Lewis.**

95) Name the sitting U.S. Vice President elected President in 1836.
Answer: Martin Van Buren.

96) Name the 2 ministers who were candidates for the U.S. Presidential nomination in 1988.
Answer: Jesse Jackson and Pat Robertson.

97) In the Old Testament, which servant did Sarah select to bear her husband Abraham's child?
Answer: Hagar.

98) Name the son of Abraham and Hagar.
Answer: Ishmael.

99) In English history, what name is given to the events of 1688-89 in which James II was deposed?
Answer: Glorious Revolution (or Bloodless Revolution; or Glorious '88).

100) Which leaders from which country came to England upon the invitation of Whig and Tory leaders to replace James II?
Answer: William (III) and Mary (II) from The Netherlands.

CHAPTER FOUR

1) In 1988, a group of 50,000 people demonstrated in Washington, D.C., on the 15th anniversary of which Supreme Court decision that made abortion legal?
Answer: *Roe v. Wade.*

2) In which Southern city was Jewish factory manager Leo Frank convicted of the murder of 13-year-old Mary Phagan on April 26, 1913?
Answer: **Atlanta (Georgia).**

3) Which disappointed office seeker killed President James Garfield?
Answer: **Charles Guiteau.**

4) Which act passed by Congress on January 16, 1883, established the principle of federal employment based on merit and competitive examination?
Answer: **Pendleton Act.**

5) Identify one of the 2 U.S. states whose northern borders are formed by the Ohio River.
Answer: **West Virginia and Kentucky.**

6) Identify 2 of the 3 U.S. states whose southern borders are formed by the Ohio River.
Answer: **Ohio, Indiana, and Illinois.**

7) Which one of these geometric constructions is possible using only a compass and a straightedge: doubling a cube, doubling a given angle, or trisecting a given angle?
Answer: **Doubling a given angle.**

8) If the shorter leg of a 30°-60°-90° triangle has length 8, how long are both the longer leg and hypotenuse?
Answer: **Longer leg = 8 times the square root of 3; hypotenuse = 16.**

9) Give the meaning of the acronym NAACP.
Answer: National Association for the Advancement of Colored People.

10) The Confederate flag has flown over the Capitol of Alabama and 2 other southern Capitols since the late 1950s and early 1960s. Name the other 2 states.
Answer: Georgia and South Carolina.

11) Give the term for the "bending movement in living things caused by an outside stimulus."
Answer: Tropism.

12) Identify the imaginary lines 23° 27' north and south of the equator, part of whose names are also signs of the Zodiac.
Answer: Tropic of Cancer and Tropic of Capricorn.

13) According to the saying, what makes the heart grow fonder?
Answer: Absence.

14) Which phrase means "the beginning and the end" and is comprised of the first and last letters of the Greek alphabet?
Answer: Alpha and omega.

15) Which economic theory of maintaining high employment and controlling inflation by varying the interest rates, tax rates, and public expenditures is named after a British economist?
Answer: Keynesianism (after John Maynard Keynes).

16) Keynesianism is making a comeback thanks to a failure of which doctrine holding that changes in the money supply determine the direction of a nation's economy?
Answer: Monetarism.

17) Identify the Jesuit-run Washington, D.C., university that is the oldest Roman Catholic college in the U.S.
Answer: Georgetown.

18) Identify the first Catholic U.S. bishop, who founded Georgetown in 1789, or give the nickname of the athletic teams at this university.
Answer: Father John Carroll or the Hoyas.

19) Of which "Gang" was Jiang Qing the leader who presided over the purges during the 1966-1976 Cultural Revolution? She was the widow of Mao Tse-tung.
Answer: "Gang of Four."

20) Identify the Chinese statesman and revolutionary leader, known as the "Father of the Revolution," who headed the Kuomintang Party and became the temporary president of the Chinese republic in 1912.
Answer: Sun Yat-Sen.

21) Traditionally, how many more weeks of winter will ensue if the groundhog sees his shadow on February 2?
Answer: 6 weeks.

22) Which states are the homes of the famous groundhogs called Punxsutawney Phil and General Lee?
Answer: Pennsylvania and Georgia.

23) Identify the distinguished chief justice of the U.S. Supreme Court nicknamed "Silver Heels" and the "Great Chief Justice." He was appointed by President Adams to head the court in 1801.
Answer: John Marshall.

24) Which chief justice of the U.S. Supreme Court appointed by President Lincoln in 1864 presided over the impeachment trial of Andrew Johnson in 1868?
Answer: Salmon Portland Chase.

25) Which country consists of one large island plus the smaller islands of Quemoy and Matsu and some smaller islets?
Answer: Taiwan.

26) Identify the world's largest sea according to most sources. Taiwan is located in this body of water.
Answer: South China Sea.

27) What is the value of e raised to the $i\pi$ power?
Answer: Negative 1.

28) Given a circle in a plane, what is the locus of the midpoints of all the diameters of the circle?
Answer: Point (this point is the center of the circle).

29) Which country did the U.S. attack in bombing raids as retaliation for the bombing of a West Berlin discotheque in 1986?
Answer: Libya.

30) Which one of the 2 American ironclad ships that fought March 9, 1862, at Hampton Roads, Virginia, was designated this country's first undersea National Historic Landmark in March 1987?
Answer: *Monitor.*

31) Identify the first sexually transmitted disease of pandemic proportions—one that ranges worldwide—that affects the victim's disease-fighting immune system.
Answer: AIDS.

32) Give the name for the warm, dry wind that blows down the eastern slopes of the Rocky Mountains. This wind raised the temperature in minutes at the Olympic venues in Calgary.
Answer: Chinook.

33) According to a popular story, which Greek tragic dramatist was killed when an eagle dropped a tortoise on his bald head, mistaking it for a stone?
Answer: Aeschylus.

34) In which masterpiece by which Greek playwright is a kingdom of birds and men called Cloudcuckooland (*Nephelococcygia*)?
Answer: *The Birds* by Aristophanes.

35) Which instrument produced by the Steinway Company is known as the "Instrument of the Immortals"?
Answer: (Steinway) piano.

36) Which musical instrument derives its name from a shortened form of the Italian for "soft and loud"?
Answer: Piano (from *pianoforte*).

37) Identify the New Testament Gospel for the following: "For God so loved the world that He gave His only begotten Son, that whosoever believeth in Him should not perish, but have everlasting life."
Answer: John (3:16, as seen often on TV sportscasts).

38) Which phrase describing one's attire is derived from Daniel 9:3 and means "in a state of great mourning or remorse; repentant"?
Answer: In sackcloth and ashes.

39) Name the author of *The Decline and Fall of the Roman Empire*.
Answer: Edward Gibbon.

40) Identify the treaty signed by the Vatican and Benito Mussolini on February 11, 1929, that guaranteed an independent Vatican City.
Answer: Lateran Treaty.

41) Name the conic section formed by the path in which the planets move about the sun.
Answer: Ellipse.

42) Give both coordinates of the foci of this ellipse: $x^2/25 + y^2/16 = 1$ (*x squared over twenty-five plus y squared over sixteen equals one*).
Answer: (3,0) and (–3,0).

43) Which amendment to the U.S. Constitution abolished slavery?
Answer: 13th.

44) Which colony, founded on January 13, 1733, by James Oglethorpe was the last of the 13 colonies to be established?
Answer: Georgia.

45) In which South American country is Quayaquil the largest city by population?
Answer: Ecuador.

46) Name the 2 largest South American countries according to area.
Answer: Brazil and Argentina.

47) What is 300% of 800?
Answer: 2400.

48) If the acute interior angles of a parallelogram are 70 degrees, how many degrees are in the obtuse interior angles?
Answer: 110.

49) Identify the trophy awarded to the winning Super Bowl team.
Answer: Vince Lombardi Trophy.

50) Which Washington Redskins quarterback was named the MVP of Super Bowl XXII?
Answer: Doug Williams.

51) Which test for detecting cancer of the cervix was named after Dr. George Papanicolaou?
Answer: Pap test.

52) Patients with which "irreversible neurological disorder whose symptoms include gradual memory loss, impairment of judgment, and disorientation" can now be lodged in the first-of-its kind boarding home in Maine?
Answer: Alzheimer's disease.

53) Which novel about a Russian physician was written by author Boris Pasternak, the 1958 Nobel Prize winner in literature?
Answer: *Dr. Zhivago.*

54) Identify the English author who used the pen name Elia for many of his essays.
Answer: Charles Lamb.

55) Name the Italian composer of both *Tosca* and *Madame Butterfly*.
Answer: Giacomo Puccini.

56) Identify either the U.S. Naval Lieutenant or his Japanese bride in Puccini's *Madame Butterfly*.
Answer: Lieutenant Pinkerton or Cio-Cio San.

57) Name the king of the gods in whose honor the Olympic Games were originally held.
Answer: Zeus.

58) In which valley in western Greece were the Olympic Games originally held?
Answer: Olympia.

59) Identify the Polish patriot, known as "The Hero of Two Worlds," who was noted for the fortifications he built during the American Revolutionary War.
Answer: Thaddeus Kosciuszko.

60) Which treaty was signed February 10, 1763, ending the French and Indian War?
Answer: Treaty of Paris.

61) Which group of water-soluble vitamins includes thiamine and riboflavin?
Answer: B-complex.

62) Which fat-soluble vitamin promotes the clotting of blood and prevents hemorrhaging?
Answer: Vitamin K.

63) Which American inventor and manufacturer received a government contract for 10,000 muskets with interchangeable parts in 1799? He also invented the cotton gin.
Answer: Eli Whitney.

64) Name the 2 oldest men to serve as U.S. President.
Answer: Ronald Reagan (77) and Dwight Eisenhower (70).

65) Which country was so named because the equator passes through it?
Answer: Ecuador.

66) Name the 2 landlocked countries of South America.
Answer: Bolivia and Paraguay.

67) How big is an angle which is half of its supplement?
Answer: 60.

68) A floor has an area of 720 square feet. How many square yards of carpeting are needed to cover it?
Answer: 80 square yards.

69) In which sport did an arbitrator in 1988 find that the owners acted in collusion against free agents after the 1985 season?
Answer: Baseball.

70) Give the meaning of the initials IBM, those representing the company known as "Big Blue."
Answer: International Business Machines.

71) What is the better known name of the disease called amyotrophic lateral sclerosis?
Answer: Lou Gehrig's disease.

72) For which professional football team did 3 victims of Lou Gehrig's disease, Matt Hazeltine, Gary Lewis, and Bob Waters, play in the 1950s and 60s?
Answer: San Francisco 49ers.

73) Identify the American author of *Hans Brinker, or The Silver Skates*.
Answer: Mary Mapes Dodge.

74) Which British author using which pen name wrote *Alice in Wonderland*?
Answer: Charles Lutwidge Dodgson used the name Lewis Carroll.

75) Which German composer is known for his *Hungarian Dances*?
Answer: Johannes Brahms.

76) Which Italian composer who had once trained for the priesthood became known as *Il Prete Rosso*, or "The Red Priest"?
Answer: Antonio Vivaldi.

77) Name Israel's first great patriarch who was commanded by God to sacrifice his son.
Answer: Abraham.

78) Who said to whom in the Bible, "Am I my brother's keeper"?
Answer: Cain to God.

79) Which war ended with a cease-fire signed at Paris on January 27, 1973, effective the next day at 8:00 a.m. Saigon time?
Answer: Viet Nam War.

80) Which Indian religious leader was assassinated in New Delhi by Nathuram Vinayak Godse in January 1948?
Answer: Mohandas Gandhi (Mahatma Gandhi).

81) Who became the emperor of Japan in 1926?
Answer: Hirohito.

82) Identify the son and heir of Emperor Hirohito who succeeded his father in 1989.
Answer: Crown Prince Akihito.

83) Give the term for the annual Presidential message to the U.S. Congress.
Answer: State of the Union Message (or Address).

84) Name the only 2 U.S. Presidents who did not give State-of-the-Union speeches.
Answer: William Henry Harrison and James Garfield.

85) Which adjective derived from the name of an area of the Soviet Union is used sometimes to describe winter blasts which send temperatures plunging across Europe?
Answer: Siberian.

86) In the Russian alphabet, which initials represent Union of Soviet Socialist Republics, the official name of the Soviet Union?
Answer: C.C.C.P.

87) If a boy delivers 16 papers after school, and this is 4/5 of what his friend delivers, how many papers does the friend deliver?
Answer: 20.

88) What conic section is the result of graphing the relationship $x^2 + y^2 = 25$ (x squared plus y squared equals 25)?
Answer: Circle.

89) From which city did the NFL's Phoenix Cardinals move?
Answer: St. Louis.

90) Name the largest passenger liner ever built. Its initials are SOS.
Answer: *Sovereign of the Seas.*

91) Which exocrine gland secretes bile?
Answer: Liver.

92) Which exocrine gland secretes tears?
Answer: Lacrimal (lachrymal) gland.

93) Which playwright, the "Father of Classical Greek Tragedy," won a prize for his masterpiece the *Oresteia* two years before his death?
Answer: Aeschylus.

94) In which work by the Greek comic playwright Aristophanes is the famous line, "Co-ax, co-ax, co-ax, Brekekekek co-ax"?
Answer: *The Frogs.*

95) If all 100 senators vote in the U.S. Senate, how many votes are needed to ratify a treaty by a two-thirds vote?
Answer: 67.

96) Identify the Soviet parliament consisting of 2 houses and 1500 members, which requires a simple majority vote to ratify a treaty.
Answer: Supreme Soviet.

97) Eleven of the 12 Apostles of Jesus were from the laboring class. Name the exception, a tax collector.
Answer: Matthew.

98) Name 2 of the 3 Apostles who formed the inner circle closest to Jesus.
Answer: Peter, James (the Greater), and John.

99) Which European war ended on May 10, 1871?
Answer: Franco-Prussian War.

100) Identify the only child of King James V of Scotland. She became queen of Scotland at a week old after her father died.
Answer: Mary, Queen of Scots.

CHAPTER FIVE

1) Who created the character of James Bond?
   Answer: Ian Fleming.

2) There have been 5 actors who have played James Bond in the most successful film series. Not counting David Niven in the spy film spoof *Casino Royale*, name 2 of the other 4.
   Answer: Sean Connery, George Lazenby, Roger Moore, and Timothy Dalton.

3) Which U.S. President said, "I see one third of a nation ill housed, ill clad, and ill nourished"?
   Answer: Franklin D. Roosevelt.

4) Which Democratic senator from Wisconsin became known for his monthly Golden Fleece award for wasteful governmental spending?
   Answer: Senator William Proxmire.

5) The equator passes through Ecuador. Name the other 2 South American countries through which this imaginary line passes.
   Answer: Brazil and Colombia.

6) Name the only 2 South American countries which do not border Brazil.
   Answer: Chile and Ecuador.

7) What is the name given to 2 or more circles that lie in the same plane and have the same center?
   Answer: Concentric circles.

8) The sine of what angle less than 90 degrees equals the cosine of 35 degrees?
   Answer: 55 degrees.

9) The Centers for Disease Control, more commonly referred to as the CDC, is an agency of the Public Health Service. In which city

is the CDC located?
Answer: Atlanta.

10) Scientists at NASA's Jet Propulsion Laboratory have begun planning a robot spacecraft for a 50-year mission into deep space. In which California city is this laboratory?
Answer: Pasadena.

11) Identify the chemical substances secreted chiefly by endocrine glands and used as "chemical messengers" to help various parts of an organism function in a coordinated manner.
Answer: Hormones.

12) Give the word for those who study hormones.
Answer: Endocrinologists.

13) Which word completes the phrase, "All's fair in love and __________"?
Answer: "war."

14) Identify the playwright of *Long Day's Journey Into Night,* who is the subject of the biography *Love and Admiration and Respect.*
Answer: Eugene O'Neill.

15) If both the U.S. President and the Vice President should die or become disqualified, which official is next in the line of succession?
Answer: Speaker of the House.

16) Identify any 2 of the following: the first Secretary of the Treasury, the first Secretary of War, and the first Attorney General in the Washington administration.
Answer: Alexander Hamilton, Henry Knox, and Edmund Randolph (the first Attorney General and the 2nd Secretary of State).

17) On which date is the Epiphany?
Answer: January 6.

18) Give the traditional names for 2 of the Three Wise Men of the East, the Magi, or the Three Kings who visited Bethlehem on January 6.
Answer: Gaspar (Caspar), Melchior, and Balthazar (Balthasar).

19) In which country did a surprise witness testify in 1988 that he saw a soldier shoot Benigno Aquino as he returned from exile in August 1983?
Answer: Philippines.

20) Identify the world's 2 biggest trading partners who signed an historic trade pact in 1988.
Answer: Canada and the United States.

21) On Wall Street, what is known as the DOW?
Answer: Dow Jones industrial average.

22) What is known as an IPO when a company is taken public, or what is known as an LBO, a transaction in which a small group of investors buys a company with mostly borrowed funds?
Answer: Initial-public-offering or leveraged buyout.

23) On a front porch in Inez, Kentucky, in 1964, which President started his War on Poverty after announcing it in his State-of-the-Union Message in January of the same year?
Answer: Lyndon Johnson.

24) Which American woman, sometimes called the "Mother of the Equal Rights Amendment to the U.S. Constitution," formed the National Woman's Party in 1913?
Answer: Alice Paul.

25) Which U.S. state was admitted to the Union on January 3, 1959, as the 49th state?
Answer: Alaska.

26) In which U.S. state are the annual Paul Bunyan Sled Dog Races held in the town of Bemidji in January?
Answer: Minnesota.

27) What is 10 to the 6th power?
Answer: One million.

28) If a piece of wood weighing 12 ounces is found to have a weight of 10 ounces after drying, what fraction of the wood was moisture content?
Answer: 2/12 or 1/6.

29) Identify the youngest son of Queen Elizabeth II who resigned from the Royal Marines in 1987.
Answer: Prince Edward.

30) Give the meaning of the acronym AID, a U.S. government agency that administers most of the nation's economic and technical foreign aid programs.
Answer: Agency for International Development.

31) Which hormone is known as GH?
Answer: Growth hormone (or somatotropin).

32) Which endocrine gland produces the growth hormone?
Answer: (Anterior) Pituitary gland.

33) Identify the fictional character, created over 100 years ago, who is at the moment "in retirement in Sussex, keeping bees."
Answer: Sherlock Holmes.

34) What is Sherlock Holmes' London address?
Answer: 221B Baker Street.

35) In music, what is the meaning of the initials *R&B*?
Answer: Rhythm and Blues.

36) In music, what is the meaning of the word *chanteuse*?
Answer: Female singer (especially a nightclub singer).

37) What is the nationality of Jean Henri Dunant, the founder of the Red Cross and the winner of the first Nobel Peace Prize in 1901?
Answer: Swiss.

38) Which Alsatian-born philosopher, physician, musician, and missionary won the Nobel Peace Prize in 1952? This man established a hospital in Africa in 1913.
Answer: Albert Schweitzer.

39) Identify the cousin of Mary, Queen of Scots, who had her beheaded on February 8, 1587.
Answer: Elizabeth I.

40) Albert Schweitzer built his hospital in Lambaréné, Gabon. What name was given to the former federation of French

possessions of which Gabon became a colony before Schweitzer established his hospital there in 1913?
Answer: French Equatorial Guinea.

41) What is the numerical value of any positive number raised to the zero power?
Answer: 1.

42) If the ratio of one of the sides to the base of an isosceles triangle is 4 to 3 and the perimeter is 55 feet, what is the length of the base?
Answer: 15 feet.

43) Which future U.S. President did President Jefferson send to France in 1803 to help Robert Livingston negotiate the purchase of New Orleans? He and Livingston later made arrangements for the Louisiana purchase.
Answer: James Monroe.

44) Which U.S. President married the same woman, Rachel Robards, twice—once in 1791 before her divorce and again in 1794 after her divorce?
Answer: Andrew Jackson.

45) Which city was once divided symbolically by the Brandenburg Gate?
Answer: Berlin (into East and West Berlin).

46) Give the capitals of both West and East Germany prior to their reunification.
Answer: Bonn and East Berlin.

47) Is the square root of 2 a whole number, a rational number, or an irrational number?
Answer: An irrational number.

48) Express 1,382,000 in scientific notation.
Answer: 1.382×10^6 (1.382 times 10 to the 6th power).

49) On whose grave in Baltimore has a mysterious stranger, clad in attire black as a raven, been placing 3 red roses and a bottle of

cognac in an annual rite since 1949? This American poet is known for "Annabel Lee."
Answer: Edgar Allan Poe.

50) Name the state in which Lizzie Borden in the town of Fall River allegedly took "an ax / And gave her mother forty whacks."
Answer: Massachusetts.

51) Which gland produces the hormone insulin?
Answer: Pancreas.

52) Which endocrine gland produces a hormone that controls the metabolic rate?
Answer: Thyroid gland.

53) Which American writer, the author of *The Age of Innocence* and *Ethan Frome*, won the 1921 Pulitzer Prize for fiction?
Answer: Edith Wharton.

54) Which British poet is known for his *Childe Harold's Pilgrimage*?
Answer: (George Gordon) Lord Byron.

55) Which American songwriter composed minstrel melodies he called "Ethiopian songs" and the song "Oh! Susanna"?
Answer: Stephen Collins Foster.

56) Which Italian violinist, considered to be in league with the devil because he played so fast, had women swooning for him at every performance? He also would play on only one or two strings to show how good he was.
Answer: Niccolò Paganini.

57) In which state was Mormon leader Joseph Smith killed in the town of Nauvoo?
Answer: Illinois.

58) Which angel, according to Joseph Smith, gave him instructions for the founding of the Mormon Church?
Answer: Moroni.

59) Identify the Spanish explorer who searched for the Fountain of Youth in 1513.
Answer: Juan Ponce de Léon.

60) Identify the chancellor of Germany who was chairman of the Congress of Berlin in 1878 at which European leaders met to decide what to do with the Balkan regions controlled by Turkey.
Answer: Otto von Bismarck.

61) Which letter of our alphabet comes from the same letter as our *G*? It represented a boomerang to the Ancient Egyptians and the Greeks called it *gamma*. On a school report card it means average and in Roman numerals it means a 100.
Answer: C.

62) Which term is used in physics to designate "a number expressing the ratio of the speed of an object to the speed of the sound in the surrounding medium"?
Answer: Mach number (after Ernst Mach).

63) Which famous Civil War general died of wounds received in a battle near Chancellorsville in 1863 when his men mistook him for the enemy and shot him?
Answer: Thomas "Stonewall" Jackson.

64) On January 26, 1830, which Massachusetts senator in a speech to the U.S. Senate used the phrase, "The people's government, made for the people, made by the people, and answerable to the people"?
Answer: Daniel Webster.

65) Which European city is known as the "City of Lights"?
Answer: Paris.

66) Which remote Asian country, with which the U.S. established diplomatic relations in the 1980s, has its country's capital at Ulan Bator (Ulaanbaatar)?
Answer: Mongolia.

67) What name did mathematician R. Buckminster Fuller give to his invention of a framework of straight metal pieces networked in triangles and covered by a thin layer of aluminum or plastic?
Answer: Geodesic dome.

68) There is a square vacant lot through which children have cut a diagonal path 40 yards long. What is the whole area of the lot in square yards?
Answer: 800 square yards.

69) Which country captured the U.S.S. *Pueblo* in 1968?
Answer:　North Korea.

70) Name one of the 2 American athletes who were expelled from the Olympic Games in Mexico in 1968 for raising gloved fists in a defiant gesture as the U.S. national anthem was played.
Answer:　Tommie Smith and John Carlos.

71) Which part of the body is affected by scleroderma?
Answer:　Skin (scleroderma is defined as "hard skin").

72) In light, any color may theoretically be produced with a mixture of no more than 3 colors, known as the additive colors. What are they?
Answer:　Red, blue, and green.

73) Which Shakespearean play opens with the line, "If music be the food of love, play on!"?
Answer:　*Twelfth Night.*

74) Which phrase from which Shakespearean play means "a time of youth and inexperience"?
Answer:　"Salad days" from *Antony and Cleopatra.*

75) For which TV show was the "Funeral March of a Marionette" used as the theme song?
Answer:　*Alfred Hitchcock Presents.*

76) Which French composer is known for his whimsical "Funeral March of a Marionette"?
Answer:　Charles Gounod.

77) Name Abraham's wife who bore their son Isaac.
Answer:　Sarah.

78) On which mountain did God command Abraham to sacrifice his son Isaac?
Answer:　Mount Moriah.

79) Which country annexed Austria on March 11, 1938, more than a year prior to the start of World War II?
Answer:　Germany.

80) Give the German word for "union, especially the political union of Austria with Germany in 1938."
Answer: *Anschluss.*

81) Identify the 1948 Pulitzer Prize-winning author who wrote *Tales of the South Pacific, Hawaii,* and *Alaska.*
Answer: **James Michener.**

82) Which American artist became popular as a cover illustrator of *The Saturday Evening Post* and other magazines?
Answer: **Norman Rockwell.**

83) Identify the American aviator who flew nonstop from New York to Paris in May 1927.
Answer: **Charles A. Lindbergh.**

84) In which state at an antislavery meeting in the city of Ripon on February 28, 1854, was the name "Republican Party" proposed for a new political party?
Answer: **Wisconsin (some historians say it was in Jackson, Michigan).**

85) What is the capital of Iraq?
Answer: **Baghdad.**

86) Name the 2 rivers in Iraq along which or near which most Iraqis live and which empty into the Shatt-al-Arab before emptying into the Persian Gulf.
Answer: **Tigris and Euphrates rivers.**

87) What is the area of a rhombus whose diagonals are 8 and 10?
Answer: **40.**

88) If 2 triangles are similar and their sides are in the ratio of 2 to 3, what is the ratio of their perimeters?
Answer: **2 to 3.**

89) In 1968, in which U.S. city did Mark Rudd organize the takeover of buildings at Columbia University?
Answer: **New York City.**

90) In 1968, in which European capital did Danny the Red lead street riots?
Answer: **Paris.**

91) Which common drug whose chemical name is *acetylsalicylic acid* can help prevent heart attacks from occurring?
Answer: Aspirin.

92) What is the word for "the freezing of the dead," a process advocated by the Alcor Life Extension Foundation?
Answer: Cryonics.

93) Which type of animal featured in the title of a 1988 novel by William F. Buckley, Jr., is named Rikki Tikki Tavi in *The Jungle Book* by Rudyard Kipling?
Answer: Mongoose (*Mongoose, R.I.P.*).

94) Give the dates in the titles of 2 of the first 3 *Space Odyssey* works by Arthur C. Clarke.
Answer: *2001*, *2010*, and *2061*.

95) Which German composer and organ virtuoso, who brought baroque music to its peak, is called "The Father of Modern Music"?
Answer: Johann Sebastian Bach.

96) Which words complete each of the following titles by Johann Sebastian Bach: the *Brandenburg* _________ and the *Well-Tempered* _________?
Answer: *Concertos* and *Clavier*.

97) Identify the "Apostle to the Gentiles" who shipwrecked off the north coast of Malta in A.D. 60 or A.D. 59.
Answer: St. Paul.

98) What phrase given us by Rudyard Kipling is defined as "the supposed duty of the white peoples to manage the affairs of the underdeveloped colored races"?
Answer: White man's burden (from *The White Man's Burden*, 1899).

99) Which country did Germany invade in June 1941?
Answer: Soviet Union.

100) Name 3 of the 4 major powers during WWII that first formed an alliance known as the Allies.
Answer: United States, Great Britain, China, and the Soviet Union (by the end of the war, there were 50 countries).

CHAPTER SIX

1) Which newspaper has featured the familiar slogan "All the News That's Fit to Print" on page one since 1897?
Answer: *The New York Times.*

2) Name the first woman to be pictured on a U.S. coin in general circulation.
Answer: Susan B. Anthony (she appeared on the dollar in 1979).

3) Identify the 9th U.S. President, nicknamed "Old Tippecanoe," whose term of office lasted but 32 days.
Answer: William Henry Harrison.

4) Which former U.S. Secretary of War and senator from which state was elected provisional president of the Confederate States of America in 1861?
Answer: Jefferson Davis from Mississippi.

5) In which African country is Timbuktu?
Answer: Mali.

6) What is the capital of Mali?
Answer: Bamako.

7) How many lines can be tangent to a given circle in the plane at a given point on that circle?
Answer: One.

8) If 2 similar cylinders have radii of 3 and 4, what is the ratio of the smaller volume to the larger volume?
Answer: 27 to 64.

9) In which Ohio city is the Pro Football Hall of Fame located?
Answer: Canton.

10) Which sports are featured in the films *Breaking Away* and *Hoosiers*?
Answer: Bicycle racing and basketball.

11) Which scientist shared the Nobel Prize for physics in 1903 and won the Nobel Prize in chemistry in 1911?
Answer: Marie Curie.

12) Which scientist won the Nobel Prize in chemistry in 1954 and the Nobel Prize for peace in 1962?
Answer: Linus Pauling.

13) What does a sinologist study?
Answer: China and the Chinese.

14) Which Massachusetts governor signed a redistricting law in 1812 that divided his state into politically convenient but wildly shaped districts?
Answer: Elbridge Gerry (Gerry + salamander; a practice that is now described as *gerrymandering*).

15) Which word completes the phrase, "All that glitters is not _________"?
Answer: "gold."

16) Identify both the American artist and his famous painting of a farmer holding a pitchfork standing with his daughter.
Answer: Grant Wood and *American Gothic*.

17) Identify the gemstone of a purple or bluish-violet color which is February's birthstone.
Answer: Amethyst.

18) Identify the Roman Catholic and Anglican festival that commemorates the purification of the Virgin Mary, a festival occurring on February 2 during which time candles for sacred uses are blessed.
Answer: Candlemas Day.

19) In which country did Vidkun Quisling's name become synonymous with *traitor* because of his aid to German occupation forces during WWII?
Answer: Norway.

20) Which person speaking about which country in 1939 said, "It is a riddle wrapped in a mystery inside an enigma"?
Answer: Winston Churchill about the Soviet Union.

21) In which country did the Tet offensive in 1968 shock American public opinion?
Answer: Viet Nam.

22) In which city did riots occur at the Democratic National Convention in 1968?
Answer: Chicago (Illinois).

23) In which state did Nat Turner organize a revolt in 1831?
Answer: Virginia.

24) Who said, "Cape is go, and I am go" as he took off in his *Friendship 7* capsule on February 20, 1962, thus becoming the first American to orbit the earth?
Answer: John Glenn.

25) On which state's North Slope is oil production at Prudhoe Bay allegedly polluting the fragile tundra?
Answer: Alaska.

26) Name the U.S. city and state where "Wild Bill" Hickok became a marshal and where the Boyhood Home and Museum of Dwight D. Eisenhower are located.
Answer: Abilene, Kansas.

27) A rectangle is 40 feet long and 10 feet wide. What is the length of a side of a square which has the same area?
Answer: 20.

28) The sum of the squares of 2 consecutive positive integers is 13. Find the larger integer.
Answer: 3.

29) In which U.S. state did Rose Mofford replace Evan Mecham as governor in 1988? He was the first governor to be impeached in 59 years.
Answer: Arizona.

30) In which city in which Canadian province is the Olympic Saddledome?
Answer: Calgary, Alberta.

31) Which disease has killed more people in less time than any other disease? Fleas from infected rats spread this disease through their bites.
Answer: Black Death (a form of the bubonic plague).

32) Which #1 genetic disease is often called "65 Roses" by the children afflicted with it because the name is often too difficult for them to pronounce?
Answer: Cystic fibrosis.

33) From which Shakespearean play are the lines, "All the world's a stage, / And all the men and women merely players"?
Answer: *As You Like It.*

34) The phrase "albatross around the neck," meaning a "burden," is based upon which 1798 work by which author?
Answer: *The Rime of the Ancient Mariner* by Samuel Taylor Coleridge.

35) Which federal appeals court judge won confirmation by the U.S. Senate as the 104th justice on the Supreme Court, replacing Lewis Powell?
Answer: Anthony Kennedy.

36) Name President Reagan's first 2 choices to replace Lewis Powell on the Supreme Court. One of them was rejected by the Senate, and the other withdrew his nomination in light of the furor caused by his admission that he had used marijuana.
Answer: Robert Bork and Douglas Ginsburg.

37) Which philosophical movement in ancient Greece maintained that real knowledge of things is impossible?
Answer: Skepticism.

38) Identify the Greek philosopher who became head of the Athenian academy founded by Plato and who was a proponent of skepticism, maintaining that no absolute standard of truth exists.
Answer: Carneades.

39) Which country will control the small gambling haven of Macao until 1999?
Answer: **Portugal.**

40) In which year will China gain control of Macao?
Answer: **(December 20) 1999.**

41) What is 1/2 of 1/2 of 1/2?
Answer: **1/8.**

42) What integer does 3 cubed divided by 2 to the negative 2 power equal?
Answer: **108.**

43) Give the meaning of the initials D.C. in Washington, D.C.
Answer: **District of Columbia.**

44) Name the French architect and engineer who laid out the city of Washington, D.C. The English translation of his surname is "the child."
Answer: **Pierre L'Enfant.**

45) Which U.S. state's geographical outline forms a nearly perfect arc above Newark and Wilmington, separating it from Pennsylvania?
Answer: **Delaware's.**

46) Identify the other 2 states on which Delaware borders.
Answer: **Maryland and New Jersey.**

47) What is the cube root of 343?
Answer: **7.**

48) How many straight lines are determined by 5 different points in a plane if no 3 points are collinear?
Answer: **10.**

49) Which NHL team won its 4th Stanley Cup championship in 5 years in 1988?
Answer: **Edmonton Oilers.**

50) Identify 2 of the 3 most common statistical categories in which players in the NBA can accomplish a triple-double.
Answer: **Points, rebounds, and assists (blocked shots and turnovers sometimes replace assists).**

51) Which modern drug contains the same properties to cure fevers as the willow bark recommended by Hippocrates?
Answer: Aspirin.

52) Who was the first U.S. woman to receive a medical degree? She was born in England in 1821, and a postage stamp in her honor was issued in 1981.
Answer: Elizabeth Blackwell.

53) Give the surname of the German who collaborated with his brother Jacob to publish their *Fairy Tales*.
Answer: (Wilhelm Carl) Grimm.

54) Identify the poet who is the only American honored with a memorial bust in the Poet's Corner of Westminster Abbey.
Answer: Henry Wadsworth Longfellow.

55) Give the Italian phrase used in music for "without instrumental accompaniment."
Answer: *A cappella*.

56) Give the meaning of the Italian *con brio* as used in music.
Answer: "With spirit; with great life and vivacity."

57) Which song is known as the hymn of the Civil Rights movement?
Answer: "We Shall Overcome."

58) Give the term for "a woman who helps a couple to have a child by carrying to term an embryo resulting from insemination with the man's sperm."
Answer: Surrogate mother.

59) Which WWII leader and symbol of the Free French resistance forces served as President of the provisional government from 1944-46?
Answer: Charles de Gaulle.

60) Which king and queen of France were called "Monsieur and Madame Veto" by the Republicans because the king vetoed all decrees submitted to him?
Answer: Louis XVI and Marie Antoinette.

61) Which insect transmits the virus that causes encephalitis?
Answer: Mosquito.

62) Which disease, the first one conquered by human beings, racked Europe for several centuries and was a major killer until an English physician, Edward Jenner, developed a vaccine for it in 1796?
Answer: Smallpox.

63) Identify the amendment of 1868 that was designed to override discriminatory legislation by southern states.
Answer: 14th amendment.

64) Which U.S. Vice President killed which former secretary of the treasury in a duel in Weehawken, New Jersey, on July 11, 1804?
Answer: Aaron Burr killed Alexander Hamilton.

65) Name the world's largest bay.
Answer: Bay of Bengal.

66) Which country became in 1847 the first self-governing black republic in Africa?
Answer: Liberia.

67) Which American architect and engineer is known for his inventions of the Dymaxion Air-ocean World map and the Dymaxion house?
Answer: R. Buckminster Fuller.

68) If the hot water tap in Mary Jones' house leaks 9 ounces of water every 15 minutes, how many ounces are lost in a day?
Answer: 864 ounces.

69) Which Ohio city was chosen as the site of the Rock and Roll Hall of Fame?
Answer: Cleveland.

70) Identify the singer known as "Lady Soul," the first woman inducted into the Rock and Roll Hall of Fame.
Answer: Aretha Franklin.

71) Identify the physicist who formulated the law that says the volume of a gas at constant temperature varies inversely to

the pressure applied to the gas.
Answer: Robert Boyle.

72) Which non-contagious febrile children's disease caused by *streptococci* and often resulting in permanent heart disease made a comeback in the 1980s?
Answer: Rheumatic fever.

73) Who is the author of *Time and the River* and the subject of David Donald's biography *Look Homeward*?
Answer: Thomas Wolfe.

74) Who is the author of *O Pioneers!* and *My Antonia* and the subject of Sharon O'Brien's biography *The Emerging Voice*?
Answer: Willa Cather.

75) What is the Italian word for "a master in any art, especially a great composer, conductor, or teacher of music"?
Answer: Maestro.

76) Which most famous and acclaimed Italian conductor of the 20th century, known as "The Maestro," directed the National Broadcasting Company Symphony Orchestra from 1937 to 1954?
Answer: Arturo Toscanini.

77) In the King James version of the Bible, identify the first book of the Bible named for its hero. Is it Job, Joshua, Esther, or Ruth?
Answer: Joshua.

78) Identify the collection of Jewish religious and civil laws that consists of 2 parts, the *Mishnah* and the *Gemara*.
Answer: Talmud.

79) Which Roman of a patrician family led an unsuccessful plot against his country in 63 B.C., and was later denounced publicly before the Roman Senate?
Answer: Catiline (he was killed in 62 B.C.).

80) Which Roman publicly denounced Catiline in 4 brilliant orations entitled *In Catilinam*, almost singlehandedly foiling the conspiracy?
Answer: Cicero.

81) Which ballet dancer, known as "Misha," defected from the Soviet Union in 1974, but was invited to visit Moscow in 1988 to dance with the Bolshoi Ballet?
Answer: Mikhail Baryshnikov.

82) Name the 2 children of Prince Charles and Princess Diana. They are the second and third in line to the British throne.
Answer: Prince William and Prince Harry.

83) Who was appointed as the first black U.S. Supreme Court justice?
Answer: Thurgood Marshall.

84) Name 2 of the 4 U.S. Vice Presidents to become President upon the assassination of the President.
Answer: Andrew Johnson, Chester A. Arthur, Theodore Roosevelt, and Lyndon Johnson.

85) Identify the U.S. capital whose name is derived from the mythological bird that sprang from its ashes.
Answer: Phoenix.

86) Which railroad terminal in which city is the largest in the world?
Answer: Grand Central Station in New York.

87) Mrs. Jones expects 5 guests for dinner. In how many ways can she arrange her guests at her circular dinner table?
Answer: 24.

88) What is 5 2/5 minus 2 3/5?
Answer: 2 4/5.

89) Which U.S. President in 1977 signed a treaty that permitted Panama to take control of the canal but allowed the U.S. to defend the canal's neutrality?
Answer: Jimmy Carter (1978 when ratified).

90) In which year will Panama take control of the canal?
Answer: (December 31) 1999.

91) Which medical agency is known as the AHA?
Answer: American Heart Association (accept American Hospital Assoc.).

92) After years of steady decline, which lung disease, formerly known as consumption, is increasing in the U.S., especially among AIDS victims and the homeless?
Answer: Tuberculosis.

93) In which Shakespearean play does Ophelia sing, "Good morrow! T'is St. Valentine's Day / All in the morning betime, / And I a maid at your window, / To be your valentine"?
Answer: *Hamlet*.

94) Who is the author of *King Solomon's Mines*, *She*, and *Allan Quartermain and the Lost City of Gold*?
Answer: H. Rider Haggard.

95) Which word defined as "exemption from prosecution" was the basis of a conflict between the special prosecutor and a congressional committee chairman investigating the Iran-contra arms scandal?
Answer: Immunity.

96) Identify 2 of the 4 freedoms of which Franklin Roosevelt spoke in his message to Congress in 1941.
Answer: Of speech, of religion, from want, and from fear.

97) Give the Arabic word for the forced journey of Mohammed from Mecca to Medina in 622 A.D.
Answer: *Hegira*.

98) Give the Arabic word for "a war by Moslems against enemies of Islam, carried out as a religious duty."
Answer: *Jihad*.

99) Give the phrase for "a person brought to the American colonies under contract to work for another, usually 7 years, especially during the 17th-19th centuries."
Answer: Indentured servant.

100) The majority of black Americans trace their origin to Western Africa. Name 2 of the 3 great empires that controlled this area from about A.D. 300 to the 1500s.
Answer: Ghana, Mali, and Songhai.

CHAPTER SEVEN

1) Identify the college admissions test known by its initials SAT.
   Answer: Scholastic Aptitude Test.

2) Identify the college admissions test known as the ACT.
   Answer: American College Test.

3) Identify the organization known by its initials SCLC.
   Answer: Southern Christian Leadership Conference.

4) Give the meaning of the initials of the labor organization known as the AFL-CIO.
   Answer: American Federation of Labor-Congress of Industrial Organizations.

5) Which U.S. city's Lake Shore Drive is sometimes closed by flooding from Lake Michigan?
   Answer: Chicago's.

6) In which Middle Eastern country is the port of Haifa?
   Answer: Israel.

7) What is the least common multiple for 3, 6 and 8?
   Answer: 24.

8) If the vertex angle of an isosceles triangle is 120 degrees, what is the size of each of the other 2 angles?
   Answer: 30 degrees.

9) Name the human-powered aircraft that crossed the 74 miles between Crete and Thira in 1988. This aircraft was named after the mythological character who escaped from the Labyrinth with his son.
   Answer: *Daedalus.*

10) Which Swiss artist frequently included in his paintings his initial "P" as well as his pipe and a shape like a key—a pun in

French on his name?
Answer: Paul Klee (*clé* is the French word for "key").

11) Give the word for the "vast Russian grasslands" that extend from the southern Ukraine into central Asia.
Answer: Steppe.

12) Give the term for the "vast, nearly treeless plains of the arctic regions."
Answer: Tundra.

13) What did Robert Burns call "love's first snowdrop," or which word completes Christopher Marlowe's line, "Sweet Helen, make me immortal with a __________"?
Answer: "(A) kiss."

14) Which French artist is noted for his marble sculpture entitled *The Kiss*?
Answer: Auguste Rodin.

15) Which state did Democrat John Stennis represent in the U.S. Senate? He spent more than 40 years in the Senate—the second longest service in history—before stepping down in 1988.
Answer: Mississippi (since November 5, 1947).

16) Which state did Democrat Carl Hayden represent in the U.S. Senate? He holds the record for the longest service in the Senate, from 1927 to 1969.
Answer: Arizona.

17) Which Pope issued a bull in February 1582, correcting the Julian Calendar, then 10 days in error?
Answer: Pope Gregory (XIII; the Gregorian Calendar became effective in most countries on 10/4/1582).

18) Identify the Moscow cathedral composed of 9 churches with onion-shaped domes.
Answer: St. Basil's Cathedral.

19) Which English Puritan leader served as Lord Protector of the Realm from 1653-1658?
Answer: Oliver Cromwell.

20) After the execution of which king did Cromwell lead an army against the rebellious Irish Roman Catholics?
Answer: Charles I.

21) On which day is President's Day celebrated in the U.S.?
Answer: Third Monday in February.

22) In 1799, who eulogized which U.S. President with the words, "To the memory of the Man, first in war, first in peace, and first in the hearts of his countrymen"?
Answer: Major General Henry "Light-Horse Harry" Lee and George Washington.

23) Give the nickname of American frontiersman William Frederick Cody.
Answer: "Buffalo Bill."

24) Which Prussian soldier arrived at Valley Forge in 1778 and began drilling General Washington's infantry?
Answer: Baron von Steuben (born Friedrich Wilhelm Ludolf Gerhard Augustin).

25) Name the highest point in the Alps.
Answer: Mont Blanc.

26) Identify the highest point in Europe, located in the Caucasus Mountains.
Answer: Mount Elbrus.

27) What is the largest prime factor of 66?
Answer: 11.

28) What is the ratio in lowest terms of pecans to peanuts in a mixture which contains 16 pounds of pecans to 8 ounces of peanuts?
Answer: 32 to 1.

29) Of Botticelli, Picasso, Cézanne, or David, which one was a painter of the *quattrocento*? This term literally means the "four hundred" and is the Italian way of designating the 15th century.
Answer: Botticelli (1445-1510).

30) Sandro Botticelli is well known for his painting entitled *Primavera*. Give the English meaning of this title.
Answer: Spring or springtime.

31) Where are the plants and animals in the ocean if they are described as *benthic*?
Answer: On the bottom.

32) Give the term for the "coniferous evergreen forests of subarctic regions."
Answer: Taiga.

33) Identify the American Pulitzer Prize winning poet known for her "Renascence" and for many sonnets.
Answer: Edna St. Vincent Millay.

34) Identify the 16th century French moralist who established the personal essay as a genre of literature.
Answer: Michel de Montaigne.

35) During which civil war is André Malraux's novel *Man's Hope* set?
Answer: Spanish Civil War.

36) Which Pablo Picasso painting was created as a protest against the bombing of a Basque town by German planes aiding Francisco Franco during the Spanish Civil War?
Answer: *Guernica.*

37) Name the Greek missionary who converted Slavs to Christianity in the 9th century and after whom the Russian alphabet is named.
Answer: Saint Cyril.

38) Give the word for a small religious painting that is a representation of some sacred personage in Eastern Orthodox Churches.
Answer: Icon.

39) Who became the French premier in June 1940, arranged the armistice with Germany, and became the "chief of state" in the French government at Vichy? Because he collaborated with the Germans, he was tried for treason and convicted after the war, dying in prison at the age of 95.
Answer: Henri Philippe Pétain.

40) Which French leader chaired the Paris Peace Conference that opened in France on January 18, 1919?
Answer: Georges Clemenceau.

41) What fractional part of a day is 20 hours?
Answer: 5/6.

42) A rectangular floor has an area of 810 square feet. How many square yards of carpeting are needed to cover it?
Answer: 90 square yards.

43) Which U.S. President in 1868 was charged with "high crimes and misdemeanors" when the House of Representatives voted to impeach him?
Answer: Andrew Johnson.

44) Identify the U.S. President who narrowly escaped death in the explosion of a naval gun being tested on the U.S.S. *Princeton* in February 1844.
Answer: John Tyler.

45) Name the highest peak in the Soviet Union.
Answer: Communism Peak (or Mt. Communism).

46) Which mountains located in the Soviet Union between the Barents Sea and the Caspian Sea serve as the dividing line between Europe and Asia?
Answer: Ural Mountains.

47) How many ounces are in a gallon?
Answer: 128.

48) What is the value of the cosine of 0 degrees?
Answer: 1.

49) Which athletic shoe has a Union Jack on the side?
Answer: Reebok.

50) Which trophy in which sport is affectionately known as the "Auld Mug"?
Answer: America's Cup in yacht racing.

51) Give the full name of the acronym AIDS.
Answer: Acquired Immune Deficiency Syndrome.

52) What is the meaning of CPU in computer jargon?
Answer: Central Processing Unit.

53) Identify the controversial American author of *Tales of a Fourth Grade Nothing*.
Answer: Judy Blume.

54) Which American author wrote *The Heart is a Lonely Hunter*?
Answer: Carson McCullers.

55) Identify the room in the U.S. Capitol in Washington, D.C., that houses statues of outstanding citizens from many states.
Answer: Statuary Hall.

56) The House of Representatives met in Statuary Hall to choose which President in the contested election of 1824?
Answer: John Quincy Adams.

57) With which religion are the Five Pillars associated?
Answer: Islam or Mohammedanism.

58) Identify 2 of the 5 Pillars of Islam.
Answer: Prayer (or Salat), almsgiving (or Zakat), fasting, pilgrimage (or Hajj), and witness (or Shadada).

59) Identify the king who on December 11, 1936, abdicated the throne of England?
Answer: Edward VIII.

60) Between which 2 countries was the First Opium War of 1839-1842 fought?
Answer: China and Britain.

61) Identify the brightest star seen from Earth at night.
Answer: Sirius (accept Dog Star).

62) Give the name for the rare alignment of the Sun, the Moon, and the Earth that increases gravitational pull, causing unusually high tides everywhere.
Answer: Syzygy.

63) Who is called the "Father of the Constitution"?
Answer: James Madison.

64) Give the surnames of 2 of the following leading delegates to the Constitutional Convention of 1787 who refused to sign the U.S. Constitution: Elbridge __________, George __________, and Edmund __________.
Answer: Elbridge Gerry, George Mason, and Edmund Randolph.

65) Which Southern city known as the "Athens of the South" has a replica of the Parthenon in one of its parks?
Answer: Nashville (Tennessee).

66) Which Arizona town is said to have been named by settlers who stripped off the branches of a large pine tree and nailed an American flag to it?
Answer: Flagstaff.

67) For what positive value of x does the expression $x^2 - 1$ equal zero?
Answer: 1.

68) If the length, width, and height of a cube were doubled, by how much would the volume of the cube increase?
Answer: Eight-fold.

69) Name the former Kentucky or the Kansas coach who with 875 and 771 victories respectively are the leaders among Division I college basketball coaches.
Answer: Adolph Rupp or Phog Allen.

70) Which former coach of the Boston Celtics leads all NBA coaches with 1037 victories? He became the full-time president and general manager of the Celtics in 1966.
Answer: Red Auerbach.

71) What is the more popular name of *The North River Steamboat*? This 1807 boat, invented by Robert Fulton, was the first practical and financially successful steamboat.
Answer: *Clermont.*

72) In 1819, the first steam-powered ship crossed the ocean. Give the name of this ship with the same name as a city in the state of Georgia.
Answer: *Savannah*.

73) The Latin quotation that begins the 1987 Tower Commission report is *Quis custodiet ipsos custodes*. Which word completes its English translation, "Who will guard the __________ themselves"?
Answer: "guardians" (or "guards").

74) Identify the Roman poet known for the above citation and for his 16 biting satires. These pieces ridicule the government corruption and crime he witnessed in Rome.
Answer: Juvenal.

75) Give the date the U.S. Constitution was signed.
Answer: September 17, 1787.

76) How many combined articles and amendments does the U.S. Constitution contain?
Answer: 33 (7 articles and 26 amendments).

77) Identify the 9th month in the Muslim year, the holy month of fasting.
Answer: Ramadan.

78) By which 2 Biblical names is the Middle East's West Bank known?
Answer: Judea and Samaria.

79) Name the queen of France who allegedly said, "Qu'ils mangent de la brioche!" She was queen from 1755 to 1793 and her statement is translated as, "Let them eat cake!"
Answer: Marie Antoinette.

80) Identify the queen of England who said, "When I am dead and opened, you shall find 'Calais' lying in my heart." She was queen from 1553 to 1558.
Answer: Mary I (Tudor).

81) Identify the outstanding French pantomime artist who said "Non" in Mel Brooks' *Silent Movie*.
Answer: Marcel Marceau.

82) Name the white-faced and whimsical philosopher tramp who lives inside Marcel Marceau.
Answer: Bip.

83) Identify the secretary to Lt. Col. Oliver North who helped her boss in a cover-up and possible obstruction of justice in destroying documents.
Answer: Fawn Hall.

84) Name the personal secretary of President Nixon who insisted she had accidentally erased 18 1/2 minutes of a taped conversation between the President and a key aide 3 days after the Watergate burglary.
Answer: Rose Mary Woods.

85) Into which body of water does the Seine River empty?
Answer: English Channel.

86) Which country owns the Galapagos Islands?
Answer: Ecuador.

87) In a right triangle, what is the side opposite the right angle called?
Answer: Hypotenuse.

88) What does the tangent of minus pi equal?
Answer: Zero.

89) In which state is the Daytona 500 race held?
Answer: Florida.

90) In which Rhode Island city is the International Tennis Hall of Fame located?
Answer: Newport.

91) Name the atomic particle that has a mass of approximately one A.M.U. and is charged with one unit of positive electricity.
Answer: Proton.

92) Which 2 of the following are noble or inert gases: hydrogen, argon, oxygen, helium, and nitrogen?
Answer: Helium and argon.

93) Which word completes the following line from Shakespeare's *Julius Caesar*: "Let me have men about me that are fat; / ... / Yond ________ has a lean and hungry look; / He thinks too much; such men are dangerous"?
Answer: "Cassius."

94) Which American said, "For everything you have missed you have gained something else; and for everything you gain, you lose something else"? He made this statement in his 1841 essay "Compensation."
Answer: Ralph Waldo Emerson.

95) Which Dutch artist's works are being evaluated by the Morellian principles to test their authenticity? American and Dutch scholars disagree about the artist of 5 of the paintings now attributed to him in American museums.
Answer: Rembrandt's.

96) What name is given to the mechanical stencil process Andy Warhol created?
Answer: Silk-screen printing.

97) Which king of England cut ties with Rome in the 16th century?
Answer: King Henry VIII.

98) Which book followed by Anglicans is the basis for the doctrine, discipline, and worship in churches that developed from the Church of England?
Answer: Book of Common Prayer.

99) Name the Roman emperor who in 313 granted Christians freedom to practice their religion and in 325 called the First Nicene Council.
Answer: Constantine (I) the Great.

100) Give the name of the pact or agreement which has come to mean "the epitome of a humiliating, dishonorable act of appeasement or surrender." It was signed in 1938 in Germany.
Answer: Munich Pact or Munich Agreement.

CHAPTER EIGHT

1) Who is known for saying, "In the future everyone will be world-famous for fifteen minutes"?
   Answer: Andy Warhol.

2) Name the Washington, D.C., school that is the world's only liberal arts college for the deaf. Its students are known as the "Bisons."
   Answer: Gallaudet College.

3) Identify the 30th U.S. President who said, "If you don't say anything, you won't be called on to repeat it"?
   Answer: Calvin Coolidge.

4) For which incident in which city were Albert Parsons, August Spies, Adolph Fischer, and George Engel hanged? These men were involved in a bombing on May 4-5, 1886.
   Answer: Haymarket Square Riot in Chicago.

5) Which U.S. State has only 3 counties, Kent, New Castle, and Sussex?
   Answer: Delaware.

6) Name any 2 of the last 3 contiguous U.S. territories to become U.S. states.
   Answer: Oklahoma (11/16/1907), New Mexico (1/6/1912), and Arizona (2/14/1912).

7) What is the weight of 5 tennis balls if 3 tennis balls weigh 15 ounces?
   Answer: 25 ounces.

8) What are the numerical values of both the sine and cosine of a 30° angle?
   Answer: Sin 30° = 1/2; cos 30° = 3/2.

9) Which college was given the "death penalty" by the NCAA in 1986 and did not play any football games in 1987 or 1988?
Answer: Southern Methodist University?

10) What is the name of the official Soviet news agency?
Answer: TASS (translated as Telegraph Agency of the Soviet Union).

11) Identify the acid that Georg Stahl, a German chemist, isolated from vinegar in 1700. This acid's name comes from the Latin word for "vinegar" or "sour wine."
Answer: Acetic acid.

12) Identify the "Father of Modern Chemistry," who was guillotined in 1794.
Answer: Antoine Lavoisier.

13) Which sport plays a prominent role in Ernest Hemingway's *Death in the Afternoon*?
Answer: Bullfighting.

14) In which work by which author does the pig Napoleon represent Stalin?
Answer: *Animal Farm* by George Orwell.

15) Name the wicked siren of German literature who sat on a cliff above the Rhine River and lured sailors to shipwreck on the reefs.
Answer: Lorelei.

16) Name both the 2-headed llama or beast of Dr. Dolittle and the 2-faced god of Roman mythology.
Answer: Pushmi-Pullyu and Janus.

17) What is the word that means "a short, fictitious story illustrating a moral or religious truth"? The Biblical stories of the Prodigal Son and the Good Samaritan are examples.
Answer: Parable.

18) Identify the French philosopher who wrote *Discours de la Méthode* (*Discourse on Method*) in 1637. This person is sometimes called the "Father of Modern Philosophy."
Answer: René Descartes.

19) Which war was fought between the 2 English royal houses, the House of York and the House of Lancaster?
Answer: War of the Roses.

20) Name 3 of the 4 countries which occupied the Allied military zones into which Germany was divided in 1945 after the German surrender in WWII.
Answer: United States, France, Great Britain, and the Soviet Union.

21) Give one of the 2 French phrases for types of epilepsy, one in which there are short periods of unconsciousness but no convulsions, the other in which there are convulsions and loss of consciousness.
Answer: *Petit mal* (small illness) or *grand mal* (great ailment).

22) Give the Latin phrases used to describe first, a government "existing by fact, and not by choice or right," and, second, a government "recognized as right and lawful."
Answer: *De facto* and *de jure*.

23) Which Civil War general said, "I propose to fight it out on this line, if it takes all summer" and "The war is over—the rebels are our countrymen again"?
Answer: Ulysses Simpson Grant.

24) Name the states in which the War Between the States began on April 12, 1861, and ended on April 9, 1865.
Answer: South Carolina and Virginia.

25) What is the capital of Burma?
Answer: Rangoon.

26) Name 2 of the 5 countries on which Burma borders.
Answer: Bangladesh, India, China, Laos, and Thailand.

27) In space, what is the locus of points 10 cm from a given plane?
Answer: 2 parallel planes.

28) A dress on sale at a 33 1/3% discount is marked down to $50. What was the original price?
Answer: $75.

29) Give the Russian word for "the emperor of Russia," a word derived from the Latin word *Caesar*.
Answer: Tsar (tzar, or czar).

30) Identify the Russian newspaper whose name means "News."
Answer: *Izvestia*.

31) In which constellation of the Northern Celestial Hemisphere can the great spiral galaxies nearest to our own galaxy be seen?
Answer: Andromeda.

32) Name the 2 planets of our solar system which have no natural satellites.
Answer: Mercury and Venus.

33) Name the Greek author of *Prometheus Bound*, written about 465 B.C.
Answer: Aeschylus.

34) Name the English author of *Prometheus Unbound*, written in 1820.
Answer: Percy Bysshe Shelley.

35) Identify the stringed musical instrument that is the largest and lowest-pitched member of the violin family.
Answer: Bass (accept bass viol, a double bass, or contrabass).

36) Identify Johann Sebastian Bach's 2 famous works named for New Testament Gospels.
Answer: *St. Matthew Passion* (or *The Passion According to St. Matthew*) and *St. John Passion* (or *The Passion According to St. John*).

37) On which day does Lent begin?
Answer: Ash Wednesday.

38) Who in the King James Version of the Bible said to whom, "Get thee behind me, Satan"?
Answer: Jesus said these words to Peter (Matthew 16:23).

39) In which country did the Soviet Union use military force to restore "socialist order" in 1956?
Answer: Hungary.

40) In which country did the Soviet Union use military force to restore "socialist order" in 1968?
Answer: Czechoslovakia.

41) For what positive value of x does the expression $x^2 - 4$ equal zero?
Answer: 2.

42) What is 150% of 150?
Answer: 225.

43) Who was the first bearded U.S. President?
Answer: Abraham Lincoln.

44) Which senator of which state was assassinated by Dr. Carl Austin Weiss in 1935?
Answer: Huey Long of Louisiana.

45) Which country of 285 million people spans 11 time zones and was the world's first Communist state?
Answer: Soviet Union.

46) Identify both Europe's longest river and the lake into which it empties.
Answer: Volga River empties into the Caspian Sea.

47) In a plane, what is the locus of the midpoints of all the radii of a given circle?
Answer: Circle.

48) If a person with a 40-hour work week takes 2 weeks of vacation a year, how many hours would a person spend on the job in one year?
Answer: 2000.

49) What kind of a "snowman" is a *Yeti*?
Answer: Abominable (Snowman).

50) Translate the phrase "neophyte's serendipity" into a more common expression.
Answer: Beginner's luck.

51) Which machine, that has never been built, can continuously produce work with no energy input, or can continuously

convert heat into work?
Answer: Perpetual motion machine.

52) What were British scientists Ramsay and Travers studying in 1898 when they discovered neon?
Answer: Liquid air.

53) Name the Greek known as the "Father of Epic Poetry" and the "Father of Song."
Answer: Homer (accept the mythological Orpheus).

54) Identify the Greek known as "The Father of Comedy."
Answer: Aristophanes.

55) In which U.S. city is the Freer Gallery of Art?
Answer: Washington, D.C.

56) In which city in which country is the State Hermitage Museum?
Answer: Leningrad, Soviet Union.

57) Identify the colorful celebration held on Shrove Tuesday.
Answer: *Mardi Gras* (French for "fat Tuesday").

58) Give the German name for the pre-Lenten period of uninhibited revelry celebrated in Austria and parts of Germany.
Answer: *Fasching*.

59) In which U.S. city was the United Nations formed in 1945?
Answer: San Francisco.

60) Which British naval hero's last words at which battle were, "Thank God I have done my duty"?
Answer: Horatio Nelson at the Battle of Trafalgar.

61) Which disease develops if the pancreas secretes too little insulin?
Answer: Diabetes (mellitus).

62) Name the 2 vaccines, one in 1955 and the other in 1961, which all but wiped out polio in the U.S.
Answer: Salk and Sabin vaccines.

63) Name the agreement under which the 13 original colonies established a government of states in 1781.
Answer: Articles of Confederation.

64) When President John Kennedy officially established the Peace Corps in March 1961, who was named this organization's first director?
Answer: Sargent Shriver.

65) According to 1990 Census figures, which city is the world's most populous?
Answer: Mexico City.

66) What is the name of the largest city by population in the largest U.S. state by area?
Answer: Anchorage, Alaska.

67) How many feet are equal to 180 inches?
Answer: 15.

68) If the hot water tap in Mary's house leaks 8 ounces (or 1 cup) of water every 15 minutes, how many cups of water are lost in a day?
Answer: 96 cups.

69) Name the greatest European sculptor of the 15th century, well known for his *The Boy David* and *St. George the Dragon*.
Answer: Donatello.

70) Name the Italian painter and Dominican friar of the 15th century who completed the well-known series of frescoes for the monastery of San Marco in Florence.
Answer: Fra Angelico.

71) Name the logarithmic scale used to measure the magnitude of earthquakes.
Answer: Richter scale.

72) Which scale measures wind velocity from 0 to 17 (or 0 to 12)?
Answer: Beaufort scale.

73) In which city did Karl Marx write *Das Kapital*?
Answer: London (England).

74) In which poem by which American poet are the lines, "On desperate seas long wont to roam, / Thy hyacinth hair, thy classic face, / Thy Naiad airs have brought me home / To the glory that was Greece, / And the grandeur that was Rome"?
Answer: "To Helen" by Edgar Allan Poe.

75) Identify the German-born composer famous for his *Water Music* and *Fireworks Music* (or *Music for the Royal Fireworks*).
Answer: George Frideric Handel.

76) Identify the French impressionist who painted *Le Déjeuner sur l'Herbe*.
Answer: Edouard Manet.

77) Which prophet led the children of Israel into the Promised Land?
Answer: Joshua.

78) Which person in the Bible said to which person, "Am I a dog that thou comest to me with staves?"
Answer: Goliath said those words to David (I Samuel 17:45).

79) Name Horatio Nelson's flagship at the Battle of Trafalgar.
Answer: *Victory*.

80) Name the 2 wives Henry VIII of England had executed in the Tower of London.
Answer: Anne Boleyn and Catherine Howard.

81) In which city is Stapleton International Airport?
Answer: Denver.

82) Which 2 cities are in the name of the airport once called Friendship Airport?
Answer: Baltimore-Washington.

83) Which U.S. President won the first wartime presidential election?
Answer: James Madison (in 1812).

84) On April 4, in which year and in which city was Martin Luther King, Jr. killed?
Answer: 1968 in Memphis (Tennessee).

85) In which historic American city can people walk the Freedom Trail?
Answer: Boston.

86) Identify the body of water located between the cities of Liverpool and Dublin.
Answer: Irish Sea.

87) Which is greater: 1/2, the square root of 1/2, or .345?
Answer: 1/2.

88) If the lengths of 2 sides of a triangle are 6 and 9, then the length of the 3rd side must be greater than what number?
Answer: 3.

89) For which team was Tom Browning playing in 1988 when he pitched the 14th perfect game in major league baseball?
Answer: Cincinnati Reds.

90) Which player for which team became the first player in major-league history to hit 40 homers and steal 40 bases in one season?
Answer: Jose Canseco of the Oakland Athletics.

91) Name the lightest and simplest known atom, whose atomic number is 1.
Answer: Hydrogen.

92) Name the heaviest naturally-occurring element, whose atomic number is 92.
Answer: Uranium.

93) In which city did Anne Frank write her diary?
Answer: Amsterdam (The Netherlands).

94) In which work by which French author is the line, "Mais il faut cultiver notre jardin," translated as "But we must cultivate our garden"?
Answer: *Candide* by Voltaire.

95) Name the American artist famous for his paintings of the sea such as *The Gulf Stream.*
Answer: Winslow Homer.

96) Identify the French artist who spent 6 months in prison in 1832 for a caricature he drew of King Louis Philippe.
Answer: Honoré Daumier.

97) Name one of the 2 wives of Jacob in the Bible.
Answer: Rachel or Leah.

98) In Matthew 22:21, who said and about what subject, "Render therefore unto Caesar the things which are Caesar's; and unto God the things that are God's"?
Answer: Jesus when speaking about taxes (tribute).

99) Which 19th century Prussian statesman became the new chancellor of the new German empire through "blood and iron"? He was known as "The Iron Chancellor."
Answer: Otto von Bismarck.

100) Name 2 of the 4 main leaders who met at the Potsdam Conference in 1945.
Answer: Harry S Truman, Joseph Stalin, Winston Churchill, and Clement Atlee, who replaced Churchill.

CHAPTER NINE

1) Give the meaning of the acronym NASA.
   Answer: National Aeronautics and Space Administration.

2) In which Tennessee city is the Saint Jude Children's Research Hospital, a facility built with the help of comedian Danny Thomas?
   Answer: Memphis.

3) In 1957, into which U.S. capital did President Eisenhower send a thousand paratroopers to aid desegregation and to place the National Guard under federal control?
   Answer: Little Rock (Arkansas).

4) In which U.S. state did the Johnstown Flood of May 31, 1889, occur, killing 2,200 people?
   Answer: Pennsylvania.

5) Name the world's tallest man-made monument, which is located in St. Louis, Missouri.
   Answer: Gateway Arch (according to the 1988 Guiness Book).

6) Identify 2 of the 3 straits through which a ship must pass when traveling from the Atlantic Ocean to the Black Sea.
   Answer: Strait of Gibraltar, the Bosporus, and the Dardanelles.

7) Which computer language is Captain Grace Hopper responsible for developing?
   Answer: COBOL.

8) What is the vertex of the parabola defined by $y = x^2 - 4x + 1$ (y equals x squared minus four x plus one)?
   Answer: (2,–3).

9) Identify the professional sports league whose acronym is MSL.
Answer: Major Soccer League (formerly the MISL, Major Indoor Soccer League).

10) Which Spanish city was awarded the 1992 Summer Olympic Games?
Answer: Barcelona.

11) Identify the Russian word for "peace." This is the name of the second Soviet space station, which was first launched in 1986.
Answer: *Mir.*

12) Which astronomer from which country revolutionized scientific thought in the 16th century with his theory that placed the sun at the center of the universe?
Answer: Nicolaus Copernicus from Poland.

13) Which poet wrote "The Village Blacksmith" and "The Wreck of the Hesperus"?
Answer: Henry Wadsworth Longfellow.

14) Name the 2 writers who declined the Nobel Prize for literature, the one in 1958 who wrote *Doctor Zhivago* and the one in 1964 who wrote *The Age of Reason*.
Answer: Boris Pasternak and Jean-Paul Sartre.

15) In which Italian city is Leonardo da Vinci's *The Last Supper* on the wall of a church?
Answer: Milan.

16) Identify the mythological lovers associated with the Dardanelles. Each night he swam across the strait until he drowned in a storm, and she then drowned herself.
Answer: Hero and Leander.

17) Identify the first black soloist to sing with the Metropolitan Opera of New York City.
Answer: Marian Anderson.

18) Which group, known as the DAR, would not allow Marian Anderson to perform in Constitution Hall in Washington, D.C., in 1939 because she was black?
Answer: Daughters of the American Revolution.

19) In 1971, which country became the only one officially expelled from the United Nations?
Answer: Taiwan (Nationalist China).

20) Which Revolutionary Communist leader of which country led the famous "Long March" in 1934?
Answer: Mao Tse-tung (or Mao Zedong) of China.

21) Give the full name of the FCC. This agency was created in 1934 to regulate interstate and foreign communications.
Answer: Federal Communications Commission.

22) Which independent agency of the U.S. government is known as the SBA? This agency offers loans, counseling, and information on business management.
Answer: Small Business Administration.

23) Which President-elect was the target of an assassination attempt on February 15, 1933?
Answer: Franklin D. Roosevelt.

24) Which city's mayor, Anton J. Cermak, was killed when Giuseppe Zangara, a mentally ill bricklayer, tried to assassinate President-elect Roosevelt in Miami in 1933?
Answer: Chicago's.

25) Which waterway, a barge canal and one of the world's largest navigational projects, links the Tennessee River and the Gulf of Mexico? It was completed in 1985.
Answer: Tennessee-Tombigbee Waterway.

26) Which branch of the U.S. Army completed the Tennessee-Tombigbee Waterway after 15 years and at a cost of $2 billion?
Answer: Army Corps of Engineers.

27) What does the secant of zero equal?
Answer: One.

28) What is the sum of all numbers that are not in the domain of *y equals one divided by quantity x cubed plus x squared minus six x*?
Answer: Negative or minus one.

29) How many seconds of silence does NASA observe on the anniversary of the *Challenger* accident?
Answer: 73.

30) In which city in which state do students pause on January 28 to remember Christa McAuliffe, their city's social science teacher who died in the shuttle explosion?
Answer: Concord, New Hampshire.

31) Identify the disease once known as "the white plague." This disease, a leading killer of Americans decades ago, made a comeback in the 1980s with over 2,000 new cases reported in 1986.
Answer: Tuberculosis.

32) Which doctor implanted the first Jarvik-7, or the artificial heart, in Dr. Barney Clark in December 1982?
Answer: Dr. William DeVries.

33) Which Dr. Seuss character, whose heart may have been two sizes too small, steals Christmas?
Answer: Grinch.

34) Which of the 3 great Greek tragedians based 3 of his 7 extant plays on Oedipus and his family?
Answer: Sophocles.

35) Which play based on a "dreadful" 1911 novel by Gaston Leroux had its Broadway debut in 1988?
Answer: *The Phantom of the Opera.*

36) Which actor, known as the "Man of a Thousand Faces," starred in the 1925 film adaptation of the novel *The Phantom of the Opera*?
Answer: Lon Chaney.

37) What is the source of the ashes used on Ash Wednesday?
Answer: The burned palms blessed on Palm Sunday (from the preceding year).

38) In church liturgy, what is the meaning of the word *Quadragesima*?
Answer: The first Sunday in Lent (accept also the 40 days of Lent).

39) Which British leader used a new term when in 1941 he referred to "a vile race of quislings," adding that the new word "will carry the scorn of mankind down the centuries"?
Answer: Winston Churchill.

40) Identify the Indian religious leader who said, "Nonviolence is the first article of my faith. It is also the last article of my creed."
Answer: Mahatma Gandhi.

41) Express 1,482,000 in scientific notation.
Answer: 1.482×10^6.

42) What is the ratio in integral lowest terms of raisins to bran flakes in a mixture which contains 1/2 ounce of raisins to 8 ounces of bran flakes?
Answer: 1 to 16.

43) Identify President Carter's Director of the Office of Management and Budget who was pressured to resign for reasons of impropriety.
Answer: Bert Lance.

44) Identify the 2 White House aides whose resignations were requested by President Nixon in an attempt to protect his own skin during the Watergate controversy.
Answer: H.R. Haldeman and John Ehrlichman.

45) In which country does a wind referred to as the "Fremantle Doctor" relieve the scorching temperatures onshore and increase in strength as the summer wears on?
Answer: Australia.

46) Which 2 seas are connected by the Dardanelles?
Answer: Aegean Sea and Sea of Marmara.

47) What is the derivative of y with respect to x of $y = e^3$?
Answer: 0.

48) If $\tan x = 4/3$, what does sine $2x$ equal?
Answer: 24/25.

49) Which inductee into the Rock and Roll Hall of Fame is known as the "King of the Blues" and the "Blues Boy"? This musician's

guitar is named Lucille.
Answer: B.B. King.

50) Which inductee into the Rock and Roll Hall of Fame, known as the "Rockabilly King," wrote and recorded "Blue Suede Shoes" in 1956?
Answer: Carl Perkins.

51) Which noble gas was named from the Greek word for "new"?
Answer: Neon.

52) Which noble gas is considered by the EPA as the No. 1 radiation health risk in the U.S. because the gas is released by soil and rocks and seeps into homes?
Answer: Radon.

53) Give the pen name of the English novelist born John Anthony Burgess Wilson, the author of *Little Wilson and Big God* and *A Clockwork Orange*.
Answer: Anthony Burgess.

54) Name both the English author of the novel *The Lost Horizon* and the Himalayan mountain valley kingdom in the novel.
Answer: James Hilton and Shangri-La.

55) How many delegates signed the U.S. Constitution?
Answer: 39.

56) Name the 2 delegates to the U.S. constitutional convention who became U.S. Presidents.
Answer: George Washington and James Madison.

57) Name the personification of death as a man or shrouded skeleton holding a scythe.
Answer: The Reaper or The Grim Reaper.

58) Name 2 of the 3 people who were thrown into the fiery furnace for not obeying King Nebuchadnezzar's command to worship the golden image as related in the Book of Daniel.
Answer: Shadrach (Hananiah), Meshach (Mishael), and Abednego (Azariah).

59) In which country was guerilla leader Cesar Augusto Sandino murdered at Managua on February 21, 1934?
Answer: Nicaragua (the Sandinistas are named after him).

60) Which war officially ended on February 5, 1985, when the mayors of Rome and Carthage met in Tunis to sign a treaty of friendship 2,131 years after hostilities ceased in 146 B.C.?
Answer: (Third) Punic War (started in 149 B.C.).

61) Identify the SI or MKS unit of electrical resistance that is named after a German physicist.
Answer: Ohm.

62) Identify the unit of electrical conductance that is the reciprocal of the ohm.
Answer: Mho.

63) On February 4, 1865, with defeat almost certain, who exchanged his title—General of the Army of Northern Virginia—for a new one: Confederate General-in-Chief?
Answer: Robert E. Lee.

64) Identify both the 16th U.S. President and the state in which he was born in the town of Hodgenville.
Answer: Abraham Lincoln was born in Kentucky.

65) On which continent is Vinson Massif the highest point?
Answer: Antarctica.

66) Which 2 seas are connected by the Bosporous strait?
Answer: Sea of Marmara and Black Sea.

67) What part of a day is 18 hours?
Answer: 3/4 (or 75%).

68) What does the cosine of pi equal?
Answer: Negative one.

69) Which art term designates "a particular shade or tint of a given color"?
Answer: Hue.

70) Which art term designates "a painting in which scenes from everyday life are treated realistically"?
Answer: Genre painting.

71) Identify the disease confined to Africa and technically known as *trypanosomiasis*.
Answer: Sleeping sickness.

72) Identify the bloodsucking insect that carries the microscopic organism responsible for sleeping sickness.
Answer: Tsetse fly.

73) What is a *plebiscite*?
Answer: A vote of the people.

74) Which book specifically is a book of antonyms and synonyms?
Answer: Thesaurus.

75) Identify the George Frideric Handel oratorio famous for its "Hallelujah" chorus.
Answer: *Messiah.*

76) In Richard Wagner's opera *Siegfried*, with which woman does Siegfried fall in love after awakening her from a long sleep?
Answer: Brunnhilde.

77) How many total arms and legs are involved in a pas de deux in ballet?
Answer: 8.

78) Which composer and pianist noted for such songs as "Memories of You" and "I'm Just Wild About Harry" gave his last professional performance one week before his 99th birthday in 1982?
Answer: James Hubert "Eubie" Blake.

79) Which British leader said, "I have nothing to offer but blood, toil, tears, and sweat"?
Answer: Winston Churchill.

80) Identify the Caribbean country from which former president Jean-Claude Duvalier fled into exile in 1986 after allegedly stealing or improperly spending $120 million in public funds.
Answer: Haiti.

81) Which grotesquely deformed Englishman known better by the nickname "The Elephant Man" suffered from an affliction formerly diagnosed as neurofibromatosis?
Answer: John Merrick.

82) New research indicates that John Merrick, the "Elephant Man," probably suffered from Proteus syndrome, a grossly disfiguring disease. For which ability was Proteus, the Greek god of the sea, known?
Answer: The ability to assume various shapes.

83) Identify President Reagan's first Secretary of State, who was eased out of office in 1982. This person later wrote *Caveat*.
Answer: Alexander Haig.

84) Which U.S. President fired which General for insubordination as commander of the United Nations forces in Korea in 1951?
Answer: President Truman fired General Douglas MacArthur.

85) Identify the city where the Anglican Archbishop of Canterbury resides in Lambeth Palace.
Answer: London (he also has a residence in Canterbury, a borough in Kent, in southeastern England).

86) In which city is Malacañang Palace?
Answer: Manila.

87) If the slope of one of 2 parallel lines is 1/2, what is the slope of the other line?
Answer: 1/2.

88) How many subsets does the set (a, b, c, d) have?
Answer: 16.

89) In which country is the presidential house known as the Blue House? Roh Tae-woo was sworn in as this country's president in 1988 in the capital city of Seoul.
Answer: South Korea.

90) Which country is the setting for the film *The Last Emperor*, a film which earned 9 Oscar nominations?
Answer: China.

91) Which instrument measures air pressure?
Answer: Barometer.

92) Which instrument measures specific gravity?
Answer: Hydrometer.

93) Which Greek philosopher did Aristophanes lampoon in *The Clouds*, characterizing him as a sophist who teaches men to cheat others through cunning reasoning?
Answer: Socrates.

94) Which Greek dramatist did Aristophanes lampoon in *The Frogs*?
Answer: Euripides.

95) Identify the Greek god of wine and fertile crops honored in the festivals of fertility during which Greek comedy developed.
Answer: Dionysus.

96) Identify the Greek god of the Sun who drove his horse-drawn chariot across the sky each day.
Answer: Helios.

97) According to the Bible, in which location in Turkish Armenia did Noah's ark land after the great flood?
Answer: Mount Ararat.

98) What name is given to the voluntary contribution made by Roman Catholics to the pope? This name is partly derived from the name of the first pope of the church.
Answer: Peter's Pence.

99) To which country did Germany send the Zimmermann Telegram offering 3 lost territories in exchange for an alliance with Germany in WWI? This telegram was turned over to the U.S. in 1917.
Answer: Mexico.

100) Identify 2 of the 3 "lost territories" Germany offered Mexico in exchange for an alliance with Germany in WWI.
Answer: Texas, Arizona, and New Mexico.

CHAPTER TEN

1) Who invented the telephone?
   Answer: Alexander Graham Bell.

2) What was the first telephone message, sent on March 10, 1876, from one room to the other?
   Answer: "Mr. Watson, come here. I want you."

3) Identify the black American born Araminta Ross and known as the "Moses of Her People" because of her role as a "conductor" on the Underground Railroad.
   Answer: Harriet Tubman.

4) Which act passed in March 1941 permitted the U.S. President to transfer weapons and other supplies to any nation whose fight against the Axis aided U.S. defense?
   Answer: Lend-Lease Act.

5) What is Australia's capital?
   Answer: Canberra.

6) Identify the island state of the Australian Commonwealth.
   Answer: Tasmania.

7) How many years is 1/2 score years?
   Answer: 10.

8) Which one of these constructions is impossible using only a compass and a straightedge: doubling, bisecting, tripling, or trisecting a given angle?
   Answer: Trisecting a given angle.

9) Name the Baltimore-born "Sultan of Swat" who hit 60 home runs in 1927.
   Answer: George Herman "Babe" Ruth.

10) On February 4, 1932, which city in which state hosted the first Winter Olympic Games held in the U.S.?
Answer: Lake Placid, New York.

11) What was the first synthetic fiber, a product created by the Du Pont Company in 1938 and exhibited at the 1939 New York World's Fair?
Answer: Nylon.

12) Identify the anatomist, called the "Father of Microscopic Anatomy," who discovered capillaries on the surface of the lung and demonstrated that they connect arteries with veins.
Answer: Marcello Malpighi.

13) Name the Irish-born author of *Ulysses*.
Answer: James Joyce.

14) Identify the black poet who wrote *The Weary Blues*, *The Dream Keeper*, and *The Panther and the Lash*.
Answer: Langston Hughes.

15) Identify the leading 18th century Italian instrument maker. More than 635 of his violins are still in existence.
Answer: Antonio Stradivari.

16) Which Lithuanian-born musician, known as the "Perfect Violinist," when asked why there was no biography written about him said, "Here is my biography. I played the violin at three and gave my first concert at seven. I have been playing ever since"?
Answer: Jascha Heifetz.

17) According to Genesis 7:7, Noah's sons were married; so how many people were on Noah's Ark?
Answer: 8 (Noah, his wife, their 3 sons and the wives of the sons).

18) Name 2 of the 3 sons of Noah.
Answer: Ham, Shem, and Japheth.

19) Which Roman leader said, "I came, I saw, I conquered"?
Answer: Julius Caesar.

20) Which Roman leader said, "Delenda est Carthago," translated as "Carthage must be destroyed"?
Answer: **Cato the Elder.**

21) Which phrase containing a number describes the underdeveloped nations of the world, especially those with widespread poverty?
Answer: **Third World.**

22) Which phrase containing a number describes the major industrialized non-Communist nations?
Answer: **First World.**

23) Name one of the 2 years during which the U.S. had 3 Presidents.
Answer: **1841 or 1881.**

24) Who were chosen President and Vice President of the U.S. by the House when an Electoral College tie was broken after 36 ballots on February 17, 1801?
Answer: **Thomas Jefferson and Aaron Burr.**

25) Identify the city in Texas whose name in translation is "Body of Christ."
Answer: **Corpus Christi.**

26) Which world capital was moved from Kyoto to Edo, meaning "Estuary Gate," and in 1869 acquired a new name meaning "Eastern Capital"?
Answer: **Tokyo (Japan).**

27) 2 is 40% of what number?
Answer: **5.**

28) What is the formula for the volume of a right circular cone?
Answer: $V = 1/3\ \text{pi}\ r$ **squared** h **(or** $V = 1/3\pi r^2 h$**; where** V **= volume,** r **= radius of the base, and** h **= height of the cone).**

29) Albert De Salvo, the murderer of 13 women between 1962 and 1964, was played by Tony Curtis in a 1968 movie. By which nickname is De Salvo better known?
Answer: **"The Boston Strangler."**

30) What was the name of the FBI's first Public Enemy Number One in the 1930s? This bank robber was shot and killed outside Chicago's Biograph Theatre.
Answer: John Herbert Dillinger.

31) Give the word for the "study of insects."
Answer: Entomology.

32) Which American plant breeder and horticulturist developed the Shasta daisy, the spineless cactus, and the white blackberry, and had a potato named after him?
Answer: Luther Burbank.

33) Which London-born author's name is in the title of a thesaurus first published in 1852 and today the best-selling thesaurus in America?
Answer: Roget.

34) Identify the London-born author of *Winnie the Pooh*.
Answer: A(lan) A(lexander) Milne.

35) Give the word for "the means of halting action on a particular bill by long speeches," especially in the U.S. Senate.
Answer: Filibuster.

36) Give both the number of votes needed to pass a U.S. Senate bill if all are present and the number needed to cut off debate.
Answer: 51 and 60.

37) What is the holiest day of the Jewish calendar, occurring on the 10th of Tishri, and observed with a sunset-to-sunset fast as penance for sins committed during the past year?
Answer: Yom Kippur.

38) What is the name of the Babylonian poem composed in southern Mesopotamia about 2000 B.C. containing an account of a flood like the Biblical flood and a champion created by the gods and known as Enkidu?
Answer: Epic of Gilgamesh.

39) Give the meaning of VE in VE Day, the day that commemorates the surrender of Germany effective on May 8, 1945.
Answer: Victory in Europe.

40) Which treaty ending which war did Adolf Hitler in 1933 vow to ignore to avenge Germany's defeat?
Answer: Treaty of Versailles ending WWI.

41) What is the slope of a horizontal line?
Answer: Zero.

42) What is the sum of the solutions of the equation $x^2 - x - 3 = 0$ (x squared minus x minus three equals zero)?
Answer: One.

43) Which word completes the 1968 slogan of conspiracy, "Don't trust anyone over __________"?
Answer: "30."

44) In which year and in which city was Robert Kennedy killed?
Answer: 1968 and Los Angeles.

45) In which country is Mount Kosciusko the highest point?
Answer: Australia.

46) Name Australia's popular tourist attraction, a huge loaf-shaped rock formation about 1 1/2 miles long in the central part of the country.
Answer: Ayers Rock.

47) 15 is 20% of what number?
Answer: 75.

48) If the area of a rectangle is to remain the same when the altitude is decreased by 20%, by what fraction must the base be increased?
Answer: 1/4.

49) The inspiration behind the Great Exposition at the Crystal Palace in London in 1851 was the German-born Consort of Queen Victoria. Name him.
Answer: Prince Albert.

50) Which Italian, also called *Il Magnifico*, was a patron to a host of Renaissance artists, including da Vinci and Michelangelo?
Answer: Lorenzo de' Medici.

51) Which Greek man of science said in reference to a lever, "Give me where to stand, and I will move the earth"?
Answer: Archimedes.

52) Which German physician established bacteriology as a separate science?
Answer: Robert Koch.

53) Name the American author of *Andersonville*.
Answer: MacKinlay Kantor.

54) Name the author of *The Naked Lunch*, a writer known for his frank accounts of life as a drug addict.
Answer: William Burroughs.

55) Give the surname of Russian-born American violinist Isaac __________, who made his debut at age 11.
Answer: Stern.

56) Give the surname of Italian composer Antonio __________, who is known for 4 concertos entitled *The Four Seasons*.
Answer: Vivaldi.

57) In which U.S. state did a trombone salesman hoodwink the local folks in *The Music Man*? This state's capital is Des Moines.
Answer: Iowa.

58) Name the English composer, better known for his comic operas, who composed the music for the hymn "Onward Christian Soldiers" (1871).
Answer: Sir Arthur Seymour Sullivan.

59) Which poor European country suffered a severe famine from 1845 to 1848 when its potato crop failed because of plant disease?
Answer: Ireland.

60) Which Mexican bandit chieftain raided a U.S. city in New Mexico in March 1916, killing 17 Americans?
Answer: General Francisco "Pancho" Villa.

61) Throughout which body organ are small clusters of special cells called the islets of Langerhans scattered?
Answer: Pancreas.

62) Which hormone secreted by the alpha cells in the islets of Langerhans allows the liver to convert the substance glycogen to glucose?
Answer: Glucagon.

63) Name the 1857 Supreme Court decision that declared that no black—free or slave—could claim U.S. citizenship.
Answer: Dred Scott decision.

64) Which 1964 act bans discrimination because of a person's color, race, national origin, religion, or sex?
Answer: Civil Rights Act of 1964.

65) Which country's flag is part of the Australian flag?
Answer: Britain's Union flag or Jack.

66) On the Australian flag there is a large star for the Commonwealth. Which constellation do the other 5 stars on the flag represent?
Answer: Southern Cross.

67) What name is given to the point of concurrency of the 3 angle bisectors of a triangle?
Answer: Incenter.

68) If one cubic foot contains 8 gallons, how many gallons would be contained in a tub shaped like a rectangular solid and having dimensions 1 x 2 x 6 feet?
Answer: 96 gallons.

69) Give the name of the gold medal awarded annually by the NAACP to the black who has reached a high level of achievement in his or her field.
Answer: Spingarn Medal.

70) Which woman in Montgomery, Alabama, gained national attention when arrested in 1955 for disobeying a law that required blacks to sit or stand in the back of the bus?
Answer: Rosa Parks.

71) Name the British scientist who shares with Carl Scheele the credit for the discovery of oxygen.
Answer: Joseph Priestly.

72) In which state is the Lowell Observatory? It was founded by American astronomer Percival Lowell.
Answer: Arizona (in the city of Flagstaff).

73) Identify the Atlanta-born author of *Deliverance*.
Answer: James Dickey.

74) Which 1516 work by which English author canonized in 1935 is an account of an ideal society?
Answer: *Utopia* by Sir Thomas More.

75) Identify the former U.S. government department dealing with public health and social welfare and known as HEW.
Answer: Health, Education, and Welfare.

76) Which woman became the first secretary of HEW when President Eisenhower created the department in 1953?
Answer: Oveta Culp Hobby.

77) With which religion is the "white salamander letter" associated? This letter was one of 2 documents forged by Mark Hoffman, a man who pleaded guilty to committing 2 murders in 1985.
Answer: Mormonism.

78) In which capital city in which state does the Church of Jesus Christ of Latter Day Saints, or the Mormon Church, have its headquarters?
Answer: Salt Lake City, Utah.

79) Which British leader said, "Trust in God and keep your powder dry"?
Answer: Oliver Cromwell.

80) Which English queen said, "I know I have the body of a weak and feeble woman, but I have the heart and stomach of a king, and of a king of England too"?
Answer: Elizabeth I.

81) What phrase related to Julius Caesar's military activities means "to take a decisive step from which one cannot back down"?
Answer: To cross the Rubicon.

82) French scholar Jean François Champollion set out at age 12 to study ancient languages in order to be able to decipher which stone containing Egyptian hieroglyphics?
Answer: Rosetta Stone.

83) Who ran 3 times unsuccessfully for U.S. President, served as Secretary of State for Woodrow Wilson, founded the weekly newspaper *The Commoner* in 1901, and was nicknamed "The Great Commoner"?
Answer: William Jennings Bryan.

84) Which former U.S. President sold his 6,400-volume personal library in 1815 to re-establish the Library of Congress after it was destroyed during the War of 1812?
Answer: Thomas Jefferson.

85) Name the area in South Dakota and Nebraska called *les mauvaises terres* by French explorers who found the land bumpy, difficult to travel across, and unfit for cultivation.
Answer: Badlands.

86) Identify the Russian area extending from the Urals to the Pacific Ocean whose name is synonymous with "any undesirable locale to which one is assigned as punishment."
Answer: Siberia.

87) Which Greek mathematician said, "There is no royal road to geometry"? He is known as the "Father of Geometry."
Answer: Euclid.

88) What is the cube root of -125?
Answer: -5.

89) Which country's Albertville was awarded the 1992 Winter Olympic Games?
Answer: France's.

90) How many lifetime home runs did Babe Ruth hit?
Answer: 714.

91) Of which country was Ferdinand Marcos the president before being forced into exile?
Answer: Philippines.

92) Give the term for the length of time it takes for one-half of any number of unstable nuclei or subatomic particles to disintegrate.
Answer: Half-life.

93) What number completes the following title of Richard Henry Dana's __________ *Years Before the Mast*?
Answer: *Two.*

94) Which character's name in which novel by Harriet Beecher Stowe today refers to "any cruel taskmaster"?
Answer: Simon Legree in *Uncle Tom's Cabin*.

95) Franklin Roosevelt met with Winston Churchill in 1943 at a Presidential retreat named Shangri-La. Dwight Eisenhower met there with Nikita Khrushchev in 1959. What new name did Eisenhower give to this retreat?
Answer: Camp David (named for his grandson, David Eisenhower).

96) Name the 2 writers of the 1848 *Communist Manifesto*, or the *Manifesto of the Communist Party*.
Answer: Karl Marx and Friedrich Engels.

97) Identify the Roman procurator of Judea who tried and condemned Jesus to death.
Answer: Pontius Pilate.

98) Identify the high priest of the Jews who presided at the ecclesiastical hearing that condemned Jesus to death.
Answer: (Joseph) Caiaphas.

99) Which country did Germany invade on September 1, 1939, to start WWII?
Answer: Poland.

100) Name 2 of the 3 countries that during WWII first formed an alliance known as the Axis.
Answer: Germany, Italy, and Japan (6 countries joined later).

CHAPTER ELEVEN

1) Identify the world's first nuclear powered submarine. It was
christened and launched on January 21, 1954.
Answer: *Nautilus.*

2) Identify the 2 U.S. states whose flags bear the Confederate
battle flag.
Answer: **Georgia and Mississippi.**

3) Identify the first signer of the Declaration of Independence.
Answer: **John Hancock.**

4) Identify the first presidential nominee of the Republican Party,
who lost to James Buchanan in the 1856 election. He was
renowned for many explorations in the West and was known as
the "Pathfinder."
Answer: **John Charles Frémont.**

5) Name the largest body of fresh water located wholly in the
contiguous U.S.
Answer: **Lake Michigan.**

6) Name 3 of the 4 states surrounding Lake Michigan.
Answer: **Michigan, Wisconsin, Illinois, and Indiana.**

7) What is the greatest common divisor of 12 and 8?
Answer: **4.**

8) What is the value of x in the equation $4x/15 + 18 = 22$?
Answer: $x = 15.$

9) Which black separatist leader, who had recently broken with his
mentor Elijah Muhammed, was assassinated in New York City
in 1965?
Answer: **Malcolm X.**

10) In 1972, President Nixon became the first President to visit a country not diplomatically recognized by the U.S. Name the country he visited.
Answer: China (People's Republic of China).

11) Using the root word *hemo* meaning "blood," name the instrument used to compress bleeding blood vessels in order to stop hemorrhaging.
Answer: Hemostat.

12) Of the Black Death, smallpox, typhus, and influenza, which one generally passes from one person to another in droplets discharged from the nose and mouth but is also transmitted by casual skin contact with the dried scabs of the victims?
Answer: Smallpox.

13) Give the pseudonym of the French author of *The Red and the Black*.
Answer: Stendhal.

14) Which author, sometimes called Sweden's greatest playwright, is known for his works *The Father* and *Miss Julie*?
Answer: August Strindberg.

15) In 1979, Congress passed legislation that transferred most education programs from HEW to which new Cabinet-level department?
Answer: Department of Education.

16) Which woman, the first black to hold a Cabinet post in the U.S., served as the secretary of HUD and was the last secretary of HEW and the first secretary of HHS?
Answer: Patricia Harris.

17) What award has been won by Ragnar Frisch, Jan Tinbergen, Paul Samuelson, Simon Kuznets, Gunnar Myrdal, Milton Friedman, and James Tobin?
Answer: Nobel Prize for economics.

18) Which economic theory stresses the reduction of taxes, especially for those with a higher income?
Answer: Supply-side economics.

19) Which English Duke said, "The battle of Waterloo was won on the playing fields of Eton"?
Answer: Duke of Wellington.

20) Identify the king of Epirus who said, "Another such victory over the Romans, and we are undone."
Answer: Pyrrhus.

21) Which phrase containing a number describes the Communist and socialist nations of the world?
Answer: Second World.

22) Which hard-living singer, known as "The Pearl," had a statue honoring her unveiled in Port Arthur, Texas, in 1988?
Answer: Janis Joplin.

23) Identify the first U.S. President upon whose life an assassination attempt was made, occurring on January 30, 1835, when Richard Lawrence fired 2 shots and missed.
Answer: Andrew Jackson.

24) Give the meaning of the treaty known as INF.
Answer: Intermediate Range Nuclear Forces.

25) Name the Canadian province bordering 4 of the 5 Great Lakes.
Answer: Ontario.

26) Identify the arm of the Mediterranean Sea between the cities of Palermo and Naples.
Answer: Tyrrhenian (Tuscan) Sea.

27) In mathematics, what irrational number is used as the base for natural logarithms?
Answer: e.

28) What is the area of a circle with radius 5?
Answer: 25 pi.

29) What is the nationality of Ben Johnson, the sprinter named The 1988 Associated Press Male Athlete of the Year after he broke the world record in the 100-meter dash in 1987?
Answer: Canadian.

30) Name the goal keeper for the Edmonton Oilers who was the first black to play in the goal in the NHL Stanley Cup finals.
Answer: Grant Fuhr.

31) Name the Scottish inventor of the modern steam engine.
Answer: James Watt.

32) Identify the English blacksmith and inventor who built one of the first practical steam engines in 1712.
Answer: Thomas Newcomen.

33) Which Boston-born poet, who married his 13-year-old cousin, Virginia Clemm, wrote "The Raven" and other poems?
Answer: Edgar Allan Poe.

34) Which English author of *In Memoriam* wrote, "Ring out the old, ring in the new, / Ring, happy bells, across the snow: / The year is going, let him go; / Ring out the false, ring in the true"?
Answer: Alfred, Lord Tennyson.

35) Which French satirist and philosopher wrote *The Spirit of the Laws*?
Answer: Charles de Montesquieu.

36) Which "notorious" American filibusterer proclaimed himself the president of a new republic composed of Sonora and Baja California on January 18, 1854? In 1855, he led a successful revolution in Nicaragua.
Answer: William Walker.

37) Who is the founder of the Holy Spirit Association for the Unification of World Christianity, or the Unification Church?
Answer: The Reverend Sun Myung Moon.

38) According to the Bible, who was the wife of Uriah the Hittite, the second wife of King David, and the mother of Solomon?
Answer: Bathsheba (2 Sam 11:3; 1 Kings 1-2).

39) Which Asian leader was known as the "Romantic Revolutionary," the "Great Helmsman," and the "Founder of Communist China"?
Answer: Mao Tse-tung (or Mao Zedong).

40) Which country agreed to cede which present-day state to the
U.S. in the Adams-Onís Treaty of February 22, 1819?
Answer: Spain ceded Florida.

41) 160 is what percent of 200?
Answer: 80.

42) What is the hypotenuse of a right triangle whose legs are of
lengths 4 and 5?
Answer: The square root of 41.

43) On which battleship in Tokyo Bay were formal ceremonies
conducted by General Douglas MacArthur to mark the end of
the war with Japan on September 2, 1945?
Answer: U.S.S. *Missouri.*

44) Which English-born American wrote in which work, "These are
the times that try men's souls"?
Answer: Thomas Paine in *The American Crisis.*

45) What is the name of the only major city located on two continents—Asia and Europe—on both sides of the Bosporus?
Answer: Istanbul (Turkey).

46) Name the large African desert located in the western and
southern part of Botswana, in the northern part of South Africa,
and in the eastern part of South West Africa (Namibia).
Answer: Kalahari Desert.

47) Change 1/8 to a decimal.
Answer: .125.

48) Change 45% to both a decimal numeral and a fraction in
simplest form.
Answer: .45 and 9/20.

49) Name the first black U.S. astronaut to travel in space on August
30, 1983.
Answer: Guion S. Bluford.

50) Name the black American female poet who won a Pulitzer Prize
in 1950 for *Annie Allen*.
Answer: Gwendolyn Brooks.

51) Identify the astronaut who on May 5, 1961, became the first American in space.
Answer: Alan Shepard.

52) Name the 2 chimpanzees sent into space by the U.S. from Cape Canaveral on May 28, 1959, who became the first primates to return to earth.
Answer: Abel and Baker.

53) Give the Latin phrase for "improvised" or "for a special case only."
Answer: *Ad hoc.*

54) Give the Latin phrase for "attacking an opponent's character rather then answering his argument."
Answer: *Ad hominem* (or *argumentum ad hominem*).

55) One of the group of Russian composers known as "The Five" was the composer of the opera *Boris Godunov*. Name him.
Answer: Modest Petrovich Moussorgsky.

56) Name 2 of the other 4 in the group known as "The Russian Five."
Answer: Mili Balakirev, Nikolai Rimsky-Korsakov, César Cui, and Alexander Borodin.

57) In architecture, what is an *arc-boutant*, a striking feature of the Cathedral of Notre Dame in Paris and a characteristic generally associated with Gothic architecture?
Answer: Flying buttress.

58) Name the classical and Eastern mythological monster with the head and wings of an eagle and the body of a lion (and sometimes the tail of a serpent).
Answer: Griffin (griffon).

59) Identify the Welsh-born explorer who led the expedition to find the missing missionary-explorer, David Livingstone.
Answer: Henry Morton Stanley.

60) Between which 2 countries did President Roosevelt arrange a peace conference at Portsmouth, New Hampshire, in 1905?
Answer: Russia and Japan.

61) Which physics term designates the "force required to give to a mass of one kilogram an acceleration of one meter per second per second"?
Answer: Newton.

62) Which physics term designates the "amount of force required to give a mass of one gram an acceleration of one centimeter per second per second"?
Answer: Dyne.

63) With which U.S. President is the term Camelot associated?
Answer: John Kennedy.

64) In which state were 4 students killed at Kent State University by National guardsmen in 1970?
Answer: Ohio.

65) Which country lies at the southern tip of a continent between the Atlantic and Indian oceans?
Answer: South Africa.

66) Name 3 of the 4 continents bordering the Indian Ocean.
Answer: Africa, Asia, Australia, and Antarctica.

67) Evaluate 2 to the zero power (2^0) times 3 squared (3^2).
Answer: 9.

68) The area of a rhombus is 80. If one diagonal has length 16, what is the length of the other diagonal?
Answer: 10.

69) Who became the first modern-day major league black professional baseball player when he played for the Brooklyn Dodgers in 1947?
Answer: Jackie Robinson.

70) Name 2 of the first 5 players inducted into the Baseball Hall of Fame in 1936.
Answer: Ty Cobb, Walter Johnson, Christy Mathewson, Babe Ruth, and Honus Wagner.

71) Name the British naturalist who wrote *On the Origin of Species*.
Answer: Charles Darwin.

72) Of the Black Death, smallpox, typhoid fever, and influenza, which one is spread through contaminated food or water?
Answer: Typhoid fever.

73) Name the "King of the Elephants" in Jean and Laurent de Brunhoff's series of stories introduced in 1931 and based on a tale created by Parisian pianist Cecile Sabouraud.
Answer: Babar.

74) Give the author and the title of the symbolical moral fable in which a group of British schoolboys, shipwrecked on a tropical Pacific island, shake off their civilized behavior and revert to a state of savagery and cruelty.
Answer: William Arthur Golding's *The Lord of the Flies*.

75) Give the word for "the minimum number of members required to be present at an assembly to transact business legally."
Answer: Quorum.

76) *Beyond American Hegemony* is the title of a book. Give the meaning of the word *hegemony*.
Answer: "leadership" or "dominance."

77) Identify the Russian composer whose *Swan Lake* was neither a critical nor a public success until after his death.
Answer: Peter Ilich Tchaikovsky.

78) Identify the German and Austrian composers whose Piano Concerto No. 5 in E flat and String Quartet in C, Op. 76, #3 are both nicknamed "Emperor."
Answer: Ludwig Van Beethoven and Joseph Haydn.

79) Which wife of Henry VIII was the mother of Queen Elizabeth the First?
Answer: Anne Boleyn.

80) Identify the French king who said, "I want there to be no peasant in my realm so poor that he will not have a chicken in his pot every Sunday."
Answer: Henry IV (Henry of Navarre; Henry Bourbon).

81) In which European city is an annual January sale held at the Harrods department store?
Answer: **London.**

82) Which New England city is known for Filenes, a department store where basement bargains are eagerly sought?
Answer: **Boston.**

83) In which case did the U.S. Supreme Court rule racial segregation to be illegal in 1954?
Answer: *Brown v. Board of Education (of Topeka).*

84) Which 1896 case did the 1954 decision of *Brown v. Board of Education of Topeka* overrule?
Answer: *Plessy v. Ferguson.*

85) Which strait was called the *Hellespont* by the ancient Greeks?
Answer: **Dardanelles.**

86) Which island in which ocean is the world's 4th largest island?
Answer: **Madagascar in the Indian Ocean.**

87) What is 500% of 30?
Answer: **150.**

88) What is the length of the median drawn to the longest side of a right triangle whose hypotenuse has length 10?
Answer: **5.**

89) Which American orchestra conductor, also known as the "King of Jazz," introduced "symphonic jazz" in 1919?
Answer: **Paul Whiteman.**

90) Whose composition entitled *Rhapsody in Blue* was first performed by Paul Whiteman in 1924?
Answer: **George Gershwin.**

91) Ganymede is the largest natural satellite of a planet in the solar system. Which planet does this satellite orbit?
Answer: **Jupiter.**

92) Who is known as the "First Black Man of Science" and "the First Astronomer"? He assisted in the 1789 survey of the District of Columbia.
Answer: **Benjamin Banneker.**

93) Identify the woman in Shakespeare's *Hamlet* who was wooed by Hamlet and later went mad and drowned.
Answer: Ophelia.

94) From which Shakespearean play has come the phrase "to exact a pound of flesh," designating today "a debt harshly insisted upon"?
Answer: *The Merchant of Venice.*

95) Who was the first Jewish justice of the U.S. Supreme Court?
Answer: Louis D. Brandeis.

96) Identify the Ohio-born 25th U.S. President, who was known as the "Napoleon of Protection."
Answer: William McKinley.

97) What nickname is given to Beethoven's *Third Symphony*?
Answer: "Eroica."

98) Which Austrian composer is known for his Eighth Symphony, also called the *Symphony of a Thousand* because of the many singers and musicians needed to perform it?
Answer: Gustave Mahler.

99) Which Russian czar had the Winter Palace built in present-day Leningrad in the 1700s?
Answer: Peter the Great.

100) Identify the code of laws carved on a stone column and developed by a king who ruled Babylon for 43 years from about 1792 to 1750 B.C.
Answer: Code of Hammurabi.

CHAPTER TWELVE

1) Give the French phrase for "according to the menu" or "with a
separate price for each item on the menu."
Answer: *A la carte.*

2) Give the Italian word for "out-of-doors" or "in open air."
Answer: *Alfresco* (or *al fresco*).

3) Which branch of the U.S. armed forces was formed when the
Revenue Cutter and the Lifesaving Services were combined in
January 1915?
Answer: **Coast Guard.**

4) Name the Russian-born American known as the "Father of the
Nuclear Navy" and "Father of the Atomic Submarine." He was
forced into retirement at 83 by the Reagan administration.
Answer: **Hyman George Rickover.**

5) In which ocean is the Java Trench the deepest part?
Answer: **Indian Ocean.**

6) Name the highest point in the contiguous United States.
Answer: **Mount Whitney (in California).**

7) What's the largest prime factor of 27?
Answer: **3.**

8) If there are 1000 votes in an election and one of the 2 candidates
gets 60% of them, by how many votes does he win?
Answer: **200.**

9) Which American became the first black to win a medal in the
Winter Olympic Games when she won a bronze in figure skating
in 1988?
Answer: **Debi Thomas.**

10) Identify the first black actor to receive an Academy Award as Best Actor, doing so in the 1963 film *Lilies of the Field.*
Answer: Sidney Poitier.

11) What is the name of the imaginary line that marks the northern boundary of the Tropical Zone on a map?
Answer: Tropic of Cancer.

12) Name the point at which all 3 states of matter—solid, liquid, and gas—of a single substance exist in contact and in equilibrium with one another.
Answer: Triple point.

13) Which German is most famous for his theory of the *Ubermensch*, or "Superman," which he developed in *Thus Spake Zarathustra*?
Answer: Friedrich Nietzsche.

14) Identify the Irish author of *Man and Superman*, a play that contains the celebrated scene "Don Juan in Hell."
Answer: George Bernard Shaw.

15) Who was the U.S. President when the Washington Monument was dedicated in February 1885?
Answer: Chester A. Arthur.

16) Which senator from which state declared in February 1950 that he had documents identifying many Communist agents working in the federal government?
Answer: Joseph McCarthy from Wisconsin.

17) The model for the statue of David, thought destroyed in a fire in 1690, was discovered in 1987. Which Italian sculpted the statue of David in 1504?
Answer: Michelangelo.

18) In which city in which state is the J. Paul Getty Museum, the world's richest art museum?
Answer: Malibu, California.

19) Of which country did Baudouin, the oldest son of King Leopold III, become king in 1951? Fabiola of Spain became this country's queen in 1960.
Answer: Belgium.

20) In which country was President Syngman Rhee driven from office by student protests in 1960 after 12 years in office?
Answer: South Korea.

21) Which Indiana-born actor who starred in only 3 films died in a car accident at age 24 in 1955?
Answer: James Dean.

22) Name 2 of the only 3 films in which James Dean starred.
Answer: *East of Eden*, *Rebel Without a Cause*, and *Giant*.

23) Identify America's first state university. It was chartered in Athens in January 1785.
Answer: University of Georgia.

24) Which American wrote, "I wish the Bald Eagle had not been chosen as the Representative of our Country; he is a Bird of bad moral Character"? This person wanted the Turkey as the national symbol since he said it was a "more respectable bird."
Answer: Benjamin Franklin.

25) Name the highest point in the United States.
Answer: Mount McKinley (Alaska).

26) Name both the highest point in South America and the country in which it is located.
Answer: Mount Aconcagua in Argentina.

27) Give the next 2 terms in the sequence beginning 0,1,8,27,64...
Answer: 125 and 216.

28) Give in simplified form the cube of the binomial $(x + y)$.
Answer: $x^3 + 3x^2y + 3xy^2 + y^3$.

29) Which country lost its leader, President Mohammad Zia-ul-Haq, when his airplane crashed and exploded after it was sabotaged in 1988?
Answer: Pakistan.

30) From which country did Israel take control of the Golan Heights during a 1967 war?
Answer: Syria.

31) Which planet did Sir William Herschel discover on March 13, 1781?
Answer: Uranus.

32) Give the name in astronomy for the faintly white or colored luminous ring of light seen around a celestial body, especially the outermost portion of the sun's atmosphere.
Answer: Corona.

33) Which Paris-born English novelist wrote *Of Human Bondage*?
Answer: W. Somerset Maugham.

34) Which poet from which country wrote, "Oh wad some power the giftie gie us / To see oursels as others see us!"?
Answer: Robert Burns from Scotland.

35) Give the surname of American violinist Yehudi _________, whose autobiography is entitled *Unfinished Journey*.
Answer: Menuhin.

36) Give the surname for Israeli violinist Itzhak _________, who after an attack of polio at age 4 began walking with crutches and leg braces.
Answer: Perlman.

37) Name the mythological Titan who stole fire from Olympus and gave it to man.
Answer: Prometheus.

38) Prometheus was chained to a rock. Which part of his body was eaten by an eagle or vulture each day and renewed by Zeus each night?
Answer: Liver.

39) Which British naval hero said, "England expects every man to do his duty"?
Answer: Horatio Nelson.

40) Who said, "Power tends to corrupt and absolute power corrupts absolutely"?
Answer: Lord Acton.

41) A jacket marked down to $60 is on sale at a 33 1/3% discount. What was the original price?
Answer: $90.

42) If a grandparent divides $35,000 among 3 grandchildren in the ratio of 1:2:2, what is the least amount any child will get?
Answer: $7,000.

43) Who was nicknamed the "Hero of Fort Sumter" for his direction of the opening bombardment of the Civil War and the "Hero of Manassas" for helping win the First Battle of Bull Run?
Answer: P(ierre) G(ustave) T(outant) Beauregard.

44) Which act passed by Congress in February 1887 required American Indians to give up their tribal lands in return for citizenship and individual land grants?
Answer: Dawes Act.

45) Name the lowest point in the United States.
Answer: Death Valley (California).

46) Which building in which city is the world's tallest?
Answer: Sears Tower in Chicago.

47) If a 26-foot ladder is placed against a building 10 feet from its base, how far up the building will the ladder reach?
Answer: 24 feet.

48) Find the derivative of y with respect to x if $y = x^3$.
Answer: $y = 3x^2$ (*y equals three x squared*).

49) Which French term used in art and architecture designates "the front of a building"?
Answer: Facade.

50) Which Italian term is used in art to designate "light and dark"?
Answer: Chiaroscuro.

51) Give the name of Australia's largest bird and the world's second largest living bird, which is about 5-feet high.
Answer: Emu.

52) Identify the world's only 2 monotremes, both native to Australia.
Answer: Echidna (or spiny anteater) and duck-billed platypus.

53) The lines "Ay, tear her tattered ensign down! / Long has it waved on high, / And many an eye has danced to see / That banner in the sky" are from "Old Ironsides." Who is the American poet of those lines?
Answer: Oliver Wendell Holmes.

54) The lines "When faith is lost, when honor dies, / The man is dead!" are from "Ichabod." Who is the American poet of those lines?
Answer: John Greenleaf Whittier.

55) Name the associate justice of the U.S. Supreme Court who was the only justice ever to be impeached (1804) for *malfeasance*, or misconduct. He was acquitted the following year.
Answer: Samuel Chase.

56) Which senator from which Southern state holds the record for the longest filibuster with his 24-hour speech against a civil rights bill in 1957?
Answer: Strom Thurmond from South Carolina.

57) Which 19th century Polish composer and pianist popularized the *rubato*, or *tempo rubato*, the slowing down or speeding up of tempo for musical effect?
Answer: Frédéric François Chopin.

58) Identify the German and Russian composers whose Piano Sonata in C minor and whose Symphony No. 6 in B minor are both nicknamed "Pathètique."
Answer: Ludwig Van Beethoven and Peter Ilich Tchaikovsky.

59) Although he was not baptized until he was dying, who was the first emperor of Rome to become a Christian?
Answer: Constantine (I, or Constantine the Great).

60) Which Irish monk, who lived about A.D. 484-583, has been honored by some as the first discoverer of America?
Answer: St. Brendan (Brendan the Navigator).

61) Which term used in physics designates "an electron or positron ejected at high velocity from the nucleus of an atom undergoing beta decay"?
Answer: Beta particle.

62) Which term used in physics designates "a stream of nuclear particles traveling at very high speeds and penetrating the earth's atmosphere from outer space"?
Answer: Cosmic rays.

63) Which New England city housed the first public school in the U.S.? Classes began there in February 1635.
Answer: Boston (Boston Latin School).

64) Name both the Democratic candidate for the presidency in 1952 and 1956 and the Republican who defeated him in these election years.
Answer: Adlai Stevenson was defeated by Dwight Eisenhower.

65) Identify China's longest river.
Answer: Yangtzc Rivcr.

66) Shareworld, a theme park based on Disneyland, is on the edge of which black township in South Africa?
Answer: Soweto.

67) If a pound of meat serves 5 people, and a pound of meat costs $1.60, how much does it cost to serve 20 people?
Answer: $6.40.

68) If a girl delivers 20 papers after school, and this is 4/5 of what her friend delivers, how many papers does the friend deliver?
Answer: 25.

69) U.S. Senator Howard Baker is best remembered for saying, "What did the President know, and when did he know it?" during which hearings in 1973?
Answer: The Watergate Hearings.

70) Identify the Watergate Special Prosecutor whom President Nixon fired in the infamous Saturday Night Massacre.
Answer: Archibald Cox.

71) Identify the instrument for examining the heart and lungs by listening to the sounds they make.
Answer: Stethoscope.

72) Identify the French physician called the "Father of Chest Medicine" and the "Father of the Stethoscope."
Answer: René Théophile Hyacinthe Laënnec.

73) Identify the ancient Greek whose *Parallel Lives* served as the basis for several Shakespearean plays, including *Antony and Cleopatra*.
Answer: Plutarch.

74) Identify both Romeo's friend who is killed and Juliet's cousin who kills him in Shakespeare's *Romeo and Juliet*.
Answer: Mercutio and Tybalt.

75) What is the minimum number of seats in the House of Representatives allocated to each state?
Answer: 1.

76) In which country did American-born Elizabeth Halaby become Queen Noor (Nur) when she married King Hussein?
Answer: Jordan.

77) Identify the 19th century Russian composer of *The Nutcracker*.
Answer: Peter Ilich Tchaikovsky.

78) Identify the 19th century French composer of *Prelude to the Afternoon of a Faun*.
Answer: (Achille) Claude Debussy.

79) Identify one of the 2 men who with Marc Antony formed a triumvirate to rule the Roman Empire.
Answer: Octavius or Lepidus.

80) He was born Tafari Makonnen. He ruled as emperor of his country from 1930 until he was deposed in 1974. He was nicknamed the "Lion of Judah." What is the name of this Ethiopian emperor?
Answer: Haile Selassie (I).

81) Identify the warrior of the Chiricahua Apache Indian tribe whose Spanish name means *Jerome* and who died at Fort Sill, Oklahoma, in 1909.
Answer: Geronimo.

82) After whom was the second oldest college in the U.S. named? This Virginia college was founded in 1693.
Answer: King William III and Queen Mary II (of England).

83) Give the name for the movement during the 1800s whose aim was to end slavery.
Answer: Abolitionist movement.

84) What U.S. President was known for his "New Freedom" domestic programs?
Answer: Woodrow Wilson.

85) Into which ocean does the Orange River in Africa empty?
Answer: Atlantic Ocean.

86) Identify China's 2nd longest river, one that has the same name as a primary color.
Answer: Yellow River (also called *Huang Ho,* or *Hwang Ho*).

87) Identify the plane region bounded by 2 radii of a circle and the arc of the circle.
Answer: Sector (of a circle).

88) The scale of a map is 1/3 inch equals 50 miles. If 2 cities are 300 miles apart, how many inches apart are they on the map?
Answer: 2 inches.

89) In 1988, Israel sentenced John Demjanjuk to hang for his war crimes. By what other name is this brutal Nazi death camp guard known?
Answer: "Ivan the Terrible."

90) Identify the architect of Nazi leader Adolf Hitler's "Final Solution" against Jews, who was hanged in Israel in 1962.
Answer: Adolf Eichmann.

91) Give the name for the gas burner used for heating substances in scientific laboratories and named after a German inventor.
Answer: Bunsen Burner.

92) Identify the Italian anatomist, a pioneer in electrophysiology, who used an electrical charge to stimulate the muscular twitching of frogs in his experiments.
Answer: Luigi Galvani.

93) What does a *philatelist* collect?
Answer: Stamps.

94) What term is used to name the literary peculiarity represented by the sentence "A Man, a Plan, a Canal, Panama"?
Answer: Palindrome (spelled the same backwards and forwards).

95) Which process is defined as "the turning over of an alleged criminal by one country to another"?
Answer: Extradition.

96) How many members are in the U.S. House of Representatives?
Answer: 435.

97) Who is the patron saint of Ireland?
Answer: St. Patrick.

98) Identify the French-born author of *Institutes of the Christian Religion* who was the dominant personality in Geneva from 1541 until his death. He was one of the chief leaders of the Protestant Reformation.
Answer: John Calvin.

99) Identify the person known as the "George Washington of South America" and the "Liberator (*El Libertador*) of South America."
Answer: Simón Bolívar.

100) Give the month, day, and year on which Julius Caesar was assassinated. This day is known as the Ides of March.
Answer: March 15, 44 B.C.

CHAPTER THIRTEEN

1) The words of a well-known song's first line might be changed to "Scintillate, scintillate, asteroid minific." Give the second line of this song.
Answer: **"How I wonder where you are" (which follows "Twinkle, twinkle, little star").**

2) What name was given to March 8, 1988, the day many primary elections were held in the South?
Answer: **Super Tuesday.**

3) In which year did Wendell Willkie lose the presidential election to Franklin Roosevelt, failing to prevent FDR from winning a 3rd term?
Answer: **1940.**

4) The oldest U.S. Vice President to be inaugurated served under Harry S Truman from 1949 to 1953. Name him.
Answer: **Alben Barkley.**

5) Of which Asian country is Kuala Lumpur the capital?
Answer: **Malaysia.**

6) Malaysia consists of 2 regions about 400 miles apart separated by a sea. Name this sea.
Answer: **South China Sea.**

7) Identify the plane region bounded by an arc of a circle and the chord of that arc.
Answer: **Segment (of a circle).**

8) Find the product of the value of the sine of a 90° angle and the value of the sine of a 180° angle.
Answer: **0.**

9) Name the former manager of the Baltimore Orioles who became the first ever to manage 2 of his sons in the major leagues.
Answer: **Cal Ripken, Sr.**

10) Which race held in which state is known as the "Last Great Race on Earth"? Susan Butcher captured this race for the 4th consecutive time in 1990.
Answer: The Iditarod Trail Sled Dog Race in Alaska.

11) Name the 17th century Englishman who discovered how blood circulates in the human body.
Answer: William Harvey.

12) Name 3 of the 4 main parts of blood.
Answer: Plasma, red blood cells (erythrocytes), white blood cells (leukocytes), and platelets.

13) Give the word for "a person who is married to only one person at a time."
Answer: Monogamist.

14) Give the word for "a person who hates marriage."
Answer: Misogamist.

15) Which Austrian musician composed *The Magic Flute*?
Answer: Wolfgang Amadeus Mozart.

16) Which Austrian composer's Symphony No. 3 in D minor takes one hour and 34 minutes to perform? It is the longest of all classical symphonies.
Answer: Gustav Mahler's.

17) Give the meaning of the acronym DINK, a new advertising market.
Answer: Double Income, No Kids (husband and wife working with no children, and no plans for any).

18) Identify the mental illness that affected Alexander the Great and Winston Churchill. Scientists have found that this disease, characterized by alternating periods of depression and optimism, has a genetic link.
Answer: Manic depression (accept bipolar affective disorder).

19) Identify the archbishop of Canterbury who was murdered by 4 knights of King Henry II in 1170 in the Canterbury Cathedral.
Answer: (St.) Thomas à Becket.

20) In which Asian country is the prison where 2 fellow employees of Texan H. Ross Perot were freed, thanks to the raid he masterminded? Ken Follett's *On Wings of Eagles* was based on this incident.
Answer: Iran.

21) Who portrayed George Gipp in a 1940 film about Notre Dame football coach Knute Rockne?
Answer: Ronald Reagan.

22) Complete the title of the revived 1962 film classic *The ________ Candidate*, based on a Richard Condon novel.
Answer: *Manchurian.*

23) Identify the First Lady who controlled the government as she helped her husband continue his presidency after he suffered a paralytic stroke in 1919. This period of his administration was called the "Petticoat Presidency."
Answer: Edith Wilson.

24) Complete these lines, and then tell who the speaker was: "Is life so dear or peace so sweet as to be purchased at the price of chains and slavery? Forbid it, Almighty God! I know not what course others may take, but as for me, give me liberty or give me ________."
Answer: "death" / Patrick Henry (said on 3/23/1775).

25) Of which large North Atlantic Ocean island is Godthaab the capital? Denmark administers this, the world's largest island.
Answer: Greenland.

26) Name the 4th smallest independent European country according to area. Vaduz is its capital.
Answer: Liechtenstein.

27) How many centimeters in length is 2 meters?
Answer: 200 cm.

28) In the arithmetic progression whose first term is 9 and whose common difference is –3, what is the 4th term?
Answer: 0.

29) Which organization that establishes standards for college sports is known as the NCAA?
Answer: National Collegiate Athletic Association.

30) Complete the name of the first Greek-letter society for women, *Kappa Alpha* __________. This society was founded at DePauw University in Indiana in 1870.
Answer: *Theta.*

31) Which body organ supplies the blood with oxygen and removes carbon dioxide from it?
Answer: Lungs.

32) Which German scientist discovered X-rays in 1895 and won the first Nobel Prize in physics in 1901?
Answer: William Konrad Roentgen.

33) Which character in a Shakespearean play says, "Whether 'tis nobler in the mind to suffer / The slings and arrows of outrageous fortune, / Or to take arms against a sea of troubles, / And by opposing end them"?
Answer: Hamlet.

34) The preceding lines come from Hamlet's soliloquy in which he contemplates suicide. Spell the words *preceding* and *soliloquy*.
Answer: P-R-E-C-E-D-I-N-G / S-O-L-I-L-O-Q-U-Y.

35) Identify the Austrian composer whose last and most famous symphony, No. 41 in C, is nicknamed the "Jupiter."
Answer: Wolfgang Amadeus Mozart.

36) Identify Mozart's serenade translated as *A Little Night Music* or his opera translated as *All Women Are Like That.*
Answer: *Eine Kleine Nachtmusik* or *Così Fan Tutte.*

37) Identify the American architect whose first distinctive buildings were homes designed in his famous "prairie style."
Answer: Frank Lloyd Wright.

38) Which American architect said, "Form (ever) follows function"?
Answer: Louis Sullivan.

39) Which king of France, who served from 1589 to 1610, restored peace to the country after 40 years of civil war?
Answer: Henry IV.

40) Which edict recognizing the rights of Protestants did Henry IV issue in 1598?
Answer: Edict of Nantes.

41) The sine of which acute angle equals the cosine of 40 degrees?
Answer: 50 degrees.

42) If the perimeter of a regular hexagon is 6 inches, how long is the apothem of the hexagon?
Answer: Square root of 3 over 2.

43) Name 3 of the 4 wars the U.S. military engaged in during the 19th century.
Answer: The War of 1812, the Mexican-American War, the U.S. Civil War, and the Spanish-American War.

44) In which U.S. state near Titusville was the first major oil well drilled in 1859 by Edwin L. Drake?
Answer: Pennsylvania.

45) Name one of the 2 Western U.S. states that are almost perfect rectangles.
Answer: Wyoming or Colorado.

46) Name 3 of the 4 U.S. states that meet at the same point.
Answer: Utah, Colorado, Arizona, and New Mexico.

47) Give the numerator of the simplest fraction representing the sum of 2/5 and 1/2.
Answer: 9.

48) A shirt is priced at $19.45 less a 20% discount. How much would it cost after the discount?
Answer: $15.56.

49) Which agency of the U.S. Department of Health and Human Services is known as the FDA?
Answer: Food and Drug Administration.

50) Give the 3 letters that identify the first drug proved to prolong the lives of AIDS patients, one given Federal approval in 1987. Its full name is azidothymidine, and it is sold under the name Retrovir.
Answer: AZT.

51) Name the group of metallic elements being used in the new generation of superconductors. Their atomic numbers are 58 through 71.
Answer: Rare earths (accept lanthanide series).

52) Identify 2 of the 4 rare earths whose chemical symbols are Yb, Lu, Ce, and Eu.
Answer: Ytterbium, Lutetium, Cerium, and Europium.

53) Which animal is named *lobo* in Spanish?
Answer: Wolf.

54) What is the English meaning of the Spanish word *lluvia*?
Answer: Rain.

55) How many states had to ratify the U.S. Constitution before it could take effect?
Answer: 9.

56) Name the first 2 states to ratify the U.S. Constitution.
Answer: Delaware (Dec. 7, 1787) and Pennsylvania (Dec. 12, 1787).

57) Identify the legendary king of Asia Minor who had the power to turn everything he touched into gold.
Answer: Midas.

58) Identify the god who gave King Midas the power to turn everything into gold.
Answer: Dionysus or Dionysos (Bacchus).

59) Identify the international organization whose covenant was drawn up at Versailles in 1919 and whose headquarters was in Geneva, Switzerland. This organization was dissolved in 1946 when the United Nations replaced it.
Answer: The League of Nations.

60) Name 2 of the men who served as "Big Four" representatives at the peace negotiations in Paris at the end of WWI.
Answer: Woodrow Wilson (U.S.), Georges Clemenceau (France), David Lloyd George (England), and Vittorio Orlando (Italy).

61) Which term used in chemistry and physics designates "substances which have the same atomic number but different mass numbers"?
Answer: Isotopes.

62) Which element, whose atomic weight is about 35.5, is a mixture of 2 isotopes, one having the mass number 37, and the other, 35?
Answer: Chlorine.

63) With which U.S. administration is the term "Dollar Diplomacy" associated?
Answer: William Howard Taft's.

64) Which Kansas woman crusaded for the Anti-Saloon League using her 3 hatchets of temperance named Faith, Hope, and Charity in the early part of the 20th century?
Answer: Carrie (Carry) Nation.

65) What are the 2 names, one official and one colloquial, for the country whose capital is Amsterdam?
Answer: The Netherlands and Holland.

66) Which 2 peninsulas are separated by the Gulf of Aqaba (Akaba)?
Answer: Sinai and Arabian peninsulas.

67) What is the result when the algebraic expression n plus 7 is added to that of negative n minus 2?
Answer: 5.

68) What name is given to the Chinese puzzle made by cutting a square into 5 triangles, a square, and a parallelogram? These pieces can then be used to create other artistic arrangements.
Answer: Tangram.

69) In which specific track and field activity did the Soviet Union's Sergei Bubka set records?
Answer: Pole vaulting.

70) Identify the Georgian who was the first and only golfer to win the
Grand Slam of Golf.
Answer: Robert (Bobby) Tyre Jones, Jr.

71) Give the type of chemical reaction which occurs when 2 or more
substances combine to form one new substance.
Answer: Synthesis (accept combination).

72) Identify the largest flying land birds in North America, one of
whom became the first such bird to lay an egg in captivity, doing
so in 1988.
Answer: California condors.

73) Name the English author of *Black Beauty*, a story written to
protest cruelty to horses.
Answer: Anna Sewell.

74) Which Scottish novelist in which work wrote, "Every time a
child says, 'I don't believe in fairies' there is a little fairy
somewhere that falls down dead"?
Answer: J.M. Barrie in *Peter Pan*.

75) Give the phrase for "government appropriations for political
patronage, especially for local improvements."
Answer: Pork barrel.

76) Identify the former U.S. Secretary of State who will be long
remembered for his March 31, 1981, statement in which he said,
"As of now, I am in control here in the White House pending the
return of the Vice President."
Answer: Alexander Haig.

77) Which doctrine of the Roman Catholic Church refers to the
Virgin Mary's being free from any original sin from conception?
Answer: The Immaculate Conception.

78) Name the first 3 kings of Israel.
Answer: Saul, David, and Solomon.

79) Which Queen of England as a princess was known as "Lilibet,"
especially to her parents, the Duke and Duchess of York?
Answer: Queen Elizabeth II.

80) The phrase "Let Us Beat Swords Into Plowshares" is the motto of which world wide organization?
Answer: United Nations.

81) Which comic strip hero, created by Jerry Siegel and Joe Shuster and known as the "Man of Steel," turned 50 years old in 1988?
Answer: Superman (or Clark Kent).

82) In which city and for which newspaper does the fictional Clark Kent work?
Answer: Metropolis and the *Daily Planet*.

83) During the Civil War, which Union general led the troops at the Battle of Chattanooga and broke the Confederate line on Missionary Ridge? This general was nicknamed "Little Phil."
Answer: Philip Henry Sheridan.

84) Which Civil Rights leader in which city in 1963 is remembered for saying, "I have a dream"?
Answer: Martin Luther King, Jr., in Washington, D.C.

85) What is the English translation of the Spanish word *Rio*?
Answer: River.

86) Which Spanish word by derivation means "a saw" and designates "a range of hills or mountains"?
Answer: Sierra.

87) The final conclusion in the solving of geometric problems is designated Q.E.D. Give the meaning of Q.E.D.
Answer: *Quod erat demonstrandum* ("that is to be demonstrated").

88) If the altitude of a triangle is twice the base, and the area of the triangle is 169 square inches, how long is the base?
Answer: 13 inches.

89) Which act requires the U.S. President to inform Congress before deploying troops into hostile areas?
Answer: War Powers Act (or Resolution).

90) The War Powers Act was passed by Congress as a protest to the decisions that led to U.S. involvement in the Vietnam War. Over the veto of which President was this act passed in 1973?
Answer: Richard Nixon.

91) Which body organ filters liquid solutions and excretes them through the bladder?
Answer: Kidneys.

92) Name the process by which an animal can grow new body parts.
Answer: Regeneration.

93) Who won the 1925 Pulitzer Prize for her novel *So Big*?
Answer: Edna Ferber.

94) Which Russian author in which novel wrote, "Happy families are all alike, every unhappy family is unhappy in its own way"?
Answer: Leo Tolstoy in *Anna Karenina*.

95) Name the 9th state to ratify the Constitution, an action which put the Constitution into effect on June 21, 1788.
Answer: New Hampshire (first Congress met on March 4, 1789).

96) Name the last 2 states to ratify the Constitution.
Answer: North Carolina (Nov. 21, 1789) and Rhode Island (May 29, 1790).

97) Give the word for "a letter addressed by the Pope to his bishops on important questions." One such "letter" was Pope John XXIII's *Mater et Magistra* in 1961, which dealt with Christianity and social progress.
Answer: Encyclical.

98) Which Pope published his *Humanae Vitae* in 1968, an encyclical that reaffirmed the Roman Catholic Church's stand against artificial birth control?
Answer: Pope Paul VI.

99) Which leader developed the doctrine of *satyagraha* favoring nonviolent resistance and noncooperation in opposing British rule in India? He was called the *Mahatma* or "Great Soul" by the people of India.
Answer: Mohandas Gandhi (Mahatma Gandhi).

100) Identify the first European power to establish a beachhead on the Asian mainland, doing so in 1557.
Answer: Portugal (with Macao; Portugal will also become the last colonial power to leave).

CHAPTER FOURTEEN

1) Which New York street is synonymous with advertising despite the fact that many firms have moved elsewhere?
Answer: Madison Avenue.

2) Which London street is synonymous with journalism?
Answer: Fleet Street.

3) Identify the Pacific Ocean island on which Captain James Cook was killed in 1779.
Answer: Hawaii.

4) Name the Sierra Nevada pass in eastern California where a group of 87 settlers became snowbound in the winter of 1846-1847. Only 40 survived, and they did so by eating what they could find, including their own dead.
Answer: Donner Pass.

5) Which state capital is the largest city in area in the U.S.?
Answer: Juneau (Alaska).

6) Which state capital is the most populous of U.S. capital cities?
Answer: Phoenix (Arizona).

7) What is the probability that John gets 2 heads when he flips 2 quarters?
Answer: 1/4.

8) If a man weighing 150 pounds sits 3 feet from the center of the seesaw, how far from the center should a 75-pound boy sit to balance the seesaw?
Answer: 6 feet.

9) Give the meaning of the word *legs* in the following sentence: "*Who Framed Roger Rabbit* was given high ratings when it came

out in June 1988 and few distributors are skeptical about the movie's legs."
Answer: Staying power.

10) Identify either the leggy, buxom chanteuse in the film *Who Framed Roger Rabbit* or the actress who provides her voice.
Answer: Jessica (Rabbit), or Kathleen Turner (accept Amy Irving, who provides the singing voice of Jessica).

11) Give the 2 main ingredients for the alloy brass.
Answer: Copper and zinc.

12) Give the 2 main ingredients for the alloy bronze.
Answer: Copper and tin.

13) Give the pseudonym of the French author Marie Henri Beyle.
Answer: Stendhal.

14) Which words complete the titles of the following by French author Pierre Augustin-Caron de Beaumarchais: *The Marriage of* __________ and *The Barber of* __________?
Answer: *Figaro* and *Seville*.

15) Name the standing committee of the U.S. House of Representatives concerned with methods of raising revenue to run the government. The Senate group which does similar work is the Finance Committee.
Answer: Ways and Means.

16) In which building in which U.S. city does another flag fly higher than the U.S. flag?
Answer: United Nations in New York.

17) Which word using the root *dict-* means "an invocation of divine blessing, especially at the end of a religious service"?
Answer: Benediction.

18) Identify the U.S. President who, because he attributed his son's death in a train wreck to punishment for his sins, affirmed his loyalty to the U.S. Constitution by raising his right hand rather than swearing on the Bible at his inauguration. He was the 14th U.S. President.
Answer: Franklin Pierce.

19) In which Pacific Ocean island group did Ferdinand Magellan die in 1521?
Answer: Philippines.

20) Of which Mediterranean island did Archbishop Makarios become president in 1959?
Answer: Cyprus.

21) Which world leader became known as "Attila the Hen" and "The Iron Lady"?
Answer: Margaret Thatcher.

22) Identify both the U.S. President and the British Prime Minister who signed the Atlantic Charter during a conference aboard a cruiser off the coast of Newfoundland in August 1941.
Answer: Franklin Roosevelt and Winston Churchill.

23) Which former Civil War general declined to run for President in 1884 by saying, "If nominated, I will not accept. If elected, I will not serve"?
Answer: William Tecumseh Sherman.

24) Which 2 U.S. Presidents have won the Nobel Peace Prize?
Answer: Theodore Roosevelt and Woodrow Wilson.

25) Of which Southeast Asian nation is Vientiane the capital?
Answer: Laos.

26) Identify both the capital of Vietnam and the Vietnamese city formerly named Saigon.
Answer: Hanoi and Ho Chi Minh City.

27) How many prime numbers are there between 1 and 10?
Answer: 4 (2, 3, 5, and 7).

28) Find the area of a regular pentagon with side of length s and apothem of length 2.
Answer: $5s$.

29) Which animals are known by the name *Apis mellifera scutellata*, or in which South American country did they escape from labs in 1957?
Answer: Killer honeybees, or Brazil.

30) Which U.S. government agency is known as the USDA? Scientists in this agency have set traps and established quarantines in Mexico to prevent the killer bee swarms from reaching the U.S.
Answer: United States Department of Agriculture.

31) What is the scientific name given to the lowest temperature attainable, equal to –273.16 degrees C or –459.69 degrees F?
Answer: Absolute zero.

32) Give the term for any of several electrical devices that speed up atomic particles such as electrons and protons and give them very high amounts of energy.
Answer: Particle accelerator (accept accelerator; the betatron, cyclotron, or synchrotron are examples of this type of device).

33) Give the name derived from the Spanish word for "sweet" for the ordinary peasant girl with whom Don Quixote falls in love, believing her to be a beautiful lady.
Answer: Dulcinea.

34) Which American-born English writer in which work penned the words, "April is the cruelest month"?
Answer: T.S. Eliot in *The Waste Land*.

35) Who was the first President inaugurated under the U.S. Constitution of 1789?
Answer: George Washington.

36) In which year and in which city was George Washington inaugurated on the balcony of Federal Hall?
Answer: (April 30) 1789 in New York City.

37) The *Bhagavad Gita*, Sanskrit for "Song of the Blessed One," is a sacred text of which religion?
Answer: Hinduism.

38) Identify 2 of the 3 most important members, called the *Trimurti*, that make up Brahman, the one universal spirit in the Hindu religion.
Answer: Brahma, Vishnu, and Shiva.

39) Which German imprisoned in 1924 for his involvement with the Beer-Hall Putsch began dictating his work *Mein Kampf* to Rudolf Hess the day he entered prison?
Answer: Adolf Hitler.

40) Identify the 2 countries involved in the Falkland Islands War which started in April 1982.
Answer: Great Britain and Argentina.

41) If the slope of one of 2 perpendicular lines is 1/2, what is the slope of the other line?
Answer: –2.

42) What is the weight in ounces of 5 steel balls if 3 steel balls of the same kind weigh 225 ounces?
Answer: 375 ounces.

43) Which American statesman said, "There never was a good war or a bad peace"?
Answer: Benjamin Franklin.

44) Which American businessman and unpaid adviser to every President from Wilson to Eisenhower said, "Let us not be deceived—We are today in the midst of a cold war"?
Answer: Bernard Baruch (also quoted as, "We are in the midst of a cold war which is getting warmer").

45) Name the longest river located entirely in France.
Answer: Loire River.

46) Which 2 countries united to form the nation of Tanzania in April 1964?
Answer: Tanganyika and Zanzibar.

47) The equation $x^2 - 4x + y^2 = 6$ (*x squared minus four x plus y squared equals six*) is an equation of what type of figure?
Answer: Circle.

48) If one cubic foot contains 7.5 gallons, how many gallons would be contained in a tub shaped like a rectangular solid and measuring 1 x 2 x 6 feet?
Answer: 90 gallons.

49) Which heavyweight boxing champion is known as "Iron Mike"?
Answer: Mike Tyson.

50) Give the surname of the boxer known as "The Great John L."
Answer: Sullivan.

51) Excluding the capybara of South America, what are the world's largest rodents? There are more of these rodents in the U.S. and Canada than anywhere else in the world. This animal has a wide, flat tail that looks like a paddle.
Answer: Beavers.

52) Identify one of the 2 Indian Ocean island countries on which lemurs live naturally.
Answer: Madagascar or Comoros.

53) Which English poet wrote or in which poem is the line, "They also serve who only stand and wait"?
Answer: John Milton, or *On His Blindness*.

54) Which American poet in which poem wrote, "I celebrate myself, and sing myself"?
Answer: Walt Whitman in *Song of Myself*.

55) The U.S. Supreme Court explains its decisions in documents called *opinions*. What name is given to the opinion by one or more justices on the losing side of a decision?
Answer: Dissenting opinion.

56) What name is given to the U.S. Supreme Court opinion stated by one or more justices who vote with the majority but disagree with majority reasoning?
Answer: Concurring opinion.

57) In the first line of the authorized King James Version of the Holy Bible, what 2 things did God create "in the beginning"?
Answer: The heaven and the earth.

58) Identify 3 of the 4 places that Roman Catholics believe the soul can go to after the death of the body.
Answer: Heaven, hell, purgatory, and limbo.

59) Which group of people ruled the Romans before the establishment of the Roman republic in 509 B.C.?
Answer: Etruscans (accept Rasena, Tyrrehnoi, or Tusci).

60) Identify the 2 independent countries located within the borders of Italy.
Answer: Vatican City and San Marino.

61) Of fluorine, phosphorus, hydrogen, and gold, which one has 3 isotopes?
Answer: Hydrogen.

62) Name the 3 isotopes of hydrogen.
Answer: Protium, deuterium (or heavy hydrogen), and tritium.

63) Which person born Leslie Lynch King, Jr., became President of the U.S.?
Answer: Gerald Ford.

64) Which U.S. Presidents also served as presidents of Columbia and Princeton universities?
Answer: Woodrow Wilson and Dwight Eisenhower.

65) Which industry in 1883 developed the idea of designating 4 standard times zones in the U.S.?
Answer: Railroads.

66) In 1966, Congress passed the Uniform Time Act—calling for 6 months of daylight-saving time except in states that exempt themselves. Identify the 2 states that have exempted themselves.
Answer: Hawaii and Arizona (and parts of Indiana).

67) If 2 similar cylinders have radii of 3 and 4, what is the ratio of their lateral areas?
Answer: 9 to 16.

68) What are the solutions for $x^2 - 5x - 50 = 0$ (*x squared minus five x minus fifty equals zero*)?
Answer: $x = 10$ and $x = $ negative 5.

69) Which great master of postimpressionism said, "Nature must be treated through the cylinder, the sphere, the cone" in order "to make of impressionism something as solid and durable as the paintings in museums"? He profoundly influenced the Cubists.
Answer: Paul Cézanne.

70) Name Cézanne's former schoolmate and friend in whose *L'Oeuvre* Cézanne is represented as a restless painter and failure. This person also wrote *Nana* and *Germinal*.
Answer: Emile Zola.

71) Which 2 gases are combined in the production of ammonia?
Answer: Nitrogen and hydrogen (NH_3).

72) What is the full name of the reactions referred to as a redox system of reaction?
Answer: Reduction and oxidation.

73) Which literary device is represented by "buzz," "hiss," and "boom," words whose sounds suggest their meaning?
Answer: Onomatopoeia.

74) Name the punctuation mark used for an intentional omission, one consisting of 3 periods or asterisks.
Answer: Ellipsis.

75) Identify the acronym FDIC.
Answer: Federal Deposit Insurance Corporation.

76) Who was the youngest signer of the U.S. Constitution?
Answer: (26-year-old) Jonathan Dayton (of New Jersey).

77) In which city did the National Museum of Women in the Arts open in 1987?
Answer: Washington, D.C.

78) Identify the American painter who was a member of the French impressionist movement of the late 1800s and who is known for her paintings of mothers and children in everyday situations such as *The Bath* and *Little Girl in a Blue Armchair*.
Answer: Mary Cassatt.

79) Who is known as the "Founder and Father of Modern Communism"?
Answer: Karl Marx.

80) Identify the Spanish explorer who named Florida in March 1513 and claimed it for the king of Spain.
Answer: Juan Ponce de Léon.

81) Which American game show is known in France as *La Roue de la Fortune*?
Answer: *Wheel of Fortune.*

82) In business what is an MLP, the business structure being used to avoid paying corporate income taxes?
Answer: Master limited partnership.

83) Identify the U.S. Secretary of State who in 1973 and 1974 won worldwide acclaim for his Middle East "shuttle diplomacy."
Answer: Henry Kissinger.

84) 1968 was the year of the My Lai Massacre in Vietnam when more than 300 unarmed civilians were killed. Who was the only military man court martialed and convicted for this incident?
Answer: Lt. William L. Calley, Jr.

85) Which country is located on the Jutland Peninsula?
Answer: Denmark.

86) Identify the 3 Benelux countries.
Answer: Belgium, The Netherlands, and Luxembourg.

87) If the shorter leg of a 30°-60°-90° triangle has length 4, how long are both the longer leg and hypotenuse?
Answer: Longer leg = 4 times the square root of 3; hypotenuse = 8.

88) If C is the hypotenuse, solve the following right triangle for side A if side $B = 6$ and angle $A = 45°$.
Answer: $A = 6$.

89) Which famous baseball player from Georgia was called the "Georgia Peach"?
Answer: Tyrus Raymond Cobb (accept Ty Cobb).

90) Which boxer has appeared on the cover of *Sports Illustrated* more than any other boxer? He is known by the nickname of the "Louisville Lip."
Answer: Muhammed Ali (formerly Cassius Clay).

91) Give the term for precipitation that has been polluted by sulfur dioxide and nitrogen oxides.
Answer: Acid rain.

92) Give the common name for calcium oxide, which can be added to polluted lakes to neutralize them.
Answer: Lime.

93) In which novel by which author is the first line, "Call me Ishmael"?
Answer: *Moby Dick* by Herman Melville.

94) In which novel by which author is the first line, "Call me Jonah"?
Answer: *Cat's Cradle* by Kurt Vonnegut, Jr.

95) To which city did the U.S. government move in 1790?
Answer: Philadelphia.

96) Which 2 amendments in the Bill of Rights to the U.S. Constitution enumerate the rights of the people and provide for state power?
Answer: Amendments 9 and 10.

97) Give the word for the declarations of blessedness pronounced by Jesus in the Sermon on the Mount.
Answer: Beatitudes.

98) Name 2 of the 4 books of the Bible that have 50 or more chapters.
Answer: Genesis, Psalms, Isaiah, and Jeremiah.

99) On which Atlantic Ocean island did Napoleon die in 1821?
Answer: Saint Helena.

100) Which Pacific Ocean island was settled in 1790 by mutineers of the H.M.S. *Bounty* and some Tahitian women and men?
Answer: Pitcairn Island.

CHAPTER FIFTEEN

1) Near which city is Ben Gurion International Airport, a site named to honor the first prime minister of Israel after it became independent in 1948?
Answer: Tel Aviv.

2) Which organization was founded in 1919 by veterans of the American Expeditionary Force following WWI to improve troop morale and "to speak plainly and openly for 100% Americanism"?
Answer: American Legion.

3) Which act passed by the British Parliament in March 1765 was designed to raise funds to help support the British army stationed in America after 1763?
Answer: Stamp Act.

4) Pittsburgh-born financier Andrew Mellon served as Secretary of the Treasury under 3 U.S. Presidents. Name 2 of them.
Answer: Warren Harding, Calvin Coolidge, and Herbert Hoover.

5) Identify the country located on the Apennine Peninsula.
Answer: Italy.

6) Name the 2 countries on the Iberian Peninsula.
Answer: Spain and Portugal.

7) An ace has been drawn from a 52-card deck and not replaced. If another card is drawn, what is the chance that it will also be an ace?
Answer: 3 out of 51 or 1 in 17.

8) If a wheel rotates 12 times per minute, how many degrees does it rotate in 5 seconds?
Answer: 360 degrees.

9) Name one of the 2 golfers who have won the most Masters championships.
Answer: Jack Nicklaus (6) or Arnold Palmer (4).

10) In which city in which state is the Masters golf championship played?
Answer: Augusta, Georgia.

11) Which substance would you add to water to make a saline solution?
Answer: Salt (accept NaCl or sodium chloride).

12) Name both the process by which an atom gains one or more electrons and the opposite process by which a substance gives up electrons.
Answer: Reduction and oxidation.

13) Name the first American to win the Nobel Prize in literature, doing so in 1930. He is the author of *Main Street* and *Elmer Gantry*.
Answer: Sinclair Lewis.

14) Name the first black American to publish a book. She was also the first black American poet. In 1761, she was brought to America from Africa and purchased as a slave by a Boston merchant.
Answer: Phillis Wheatley.

15) Identify the 3 independent branches of the U.S. government.
Answer: Executive, legislative, and judicial.

16) Give any of the terms for the powers of the national government specifically listed in the Constitution.
Answer: Delegated, expressed, or enumerated powers.

17) Identify the American musician known as the "March King" who first performed "The Stars and Stripes Forever" in public in 1897.
Answer: John Philip Sousa.

18) Which composer's Piano Concerto No. 21 is known as "Elvira Madigan" because it was used in a film of the same name?
Answer: Wolfgang Amadeus Mozart.

19) In which country after 89 people were killed by Sikh extremists was a state of emergency declared in the state of Punjab by

Prime Minister Rajiv Gandhi?
Answer: India.

20) Identify the Athenian statesman and lawgiver from whose name a word used to describe any extremely harsh law or practice is derived.
Answer: Draco (adjective form is Draconian).

21) Which magician was born Ehrich Weiss in Hungary in 1874?
Answer: Harry Houdini.

22) According to some of his followers, which 16th century French astrologer predicted an earthquake caused by a "planetary alignment" in California in May 1988?
Answer: Nostradamus.

23) Identify the woman who was the first to be nominated and appointed to the U.S. Supreme Court. President Reagan nominated her in 1981.
Answer: Sandra Day O'Connor.

24) In which U.S. city in which Southern state were 9 young black men accused of raping 2 white women on a freight train on March 25, 1931?
Answer: Scottsboro, Alabama (known as the Scottsboro cases).

25) Name the Egyptian dam finished in 1970 that was designed to provide hydroelectric power to the country.
Answer: Aswan High Dam.

26) Name the lake created when the Aswan Dam was built. It was named after a former leader of Egypt.
Answer: Lake Nasser.

27) What is 5 3/5 plus 2 2/5?
Answer: 8.

28) If the lengths of 2 sides of a triangle are 6 and 9, then the 3rd side must be less than what number?
Answer: 15.

29) The School of Journalism of which university in New York City presents the Pulitzer Prizes?
Answer: Columbia University.

30) Name 2 of the 4 categories in which Pulitzer Prizes are awarded.
Answer: Journalism, literature, drama, and music.

31) How many degrees must one add in order to express a Celsius temperature reading in Kelvin?
Answer: 273 degrees.

32) A young boy walks 150 meters due east and then turns around and walks 30 meters due west. What is the boy's displacement?
Answer: 120 meters east.

33) Which work by Kenneth Grahame begins with the line, "The Mole had been working very hard all the morning, spring-cleaning his little home"?
Answer: *The Wind in the Willows*.

34) Which work by which French author opens with the line, "In the castle of Baron Thunder-ten-tronckh in Westphalia there lived a youth endowed by Nature with the most gentle character"?
Answer: *Candide* by Voltaire.

35) Which style of European art flourished from about 1520 to 1600 and was characterized by contorted figures and distortion of realistic proportions?
Answer: Mannerism.

36) The most striking Mannerist was the Spanish artist who painted *The Burial of Count Orgaz* and *View of Toledo*. What did the Spaniards call this artist born Domenikos Theotokopoulos?
Answer: El Greco.

37) Name the English-born founder of the Salvation Army.
Answer: William Booth.

38) Identify the American who was the founder of Christian Science and the Church of Christ, Scientist.
Answer: Mary Baker Eddy.

39) Identify India's first prime minister, Rajiv Gandhi's grandfather.
Answer: Jawaharlal Nehru.

40) Which war was triggered by the assassination of which archduke on June 28, 1914? This war formally ended when the Treaty of Versailles was signed on June 28, 1919.
Answer: World War I by the assassination of Francis Ferdinand.

41) What is the slope of any line parallel to the line $y - 3x - 1 = 0$ (*y minus three x minus one equals zero*)?
Answer: 3.

42) What is the hundredths digit of the decimal representation of the fraction three-sevenths?
Answer: 2.

43) Which U.S. President began withdrawing troops from the South on April 10, 1877, or what name was given to the period from 1867 to 1877 following the Civil War?
Answer: Rutherford B. Hayes or Reconstruction.

44) Which person, the first woman to sit in Congress, made her debut speech on April 6, 1917, by saying, "I want to stand by my country, but I cannot vote for war"? She also voted against U.S. entry into WWII—the only person to do so.
Answer: Jeannette Rankin.

45) In which Asian country did the volcano on the island of Krakatoa erupt in 1883 causing 36,000 deaths and creating what has been called "the loudest noise in history"?
Answer: Indonesia.

46) On which Caribbean island, an Overseas Department of France, did Mount Pelée erupt in 1902 killing all but one of the 30,000 inhabitants in the capital of Saint Pierre?
Answer: Martinique.

47) Give the mixed number for the improper fraction 40/7.
Answer: 5 5/7.

48) Give both the number of grams in 9000 milligrams and the number of meters in 4 kilometers.
Answer: 9 and 4000.

49) Which award, named after the founder of basketball, is presented to the top college player of the year?
Answer: Naismith Award.

50) Which organization in which state presents the Naismith Award?
Answer: Atlanta Tip-Off Club in Georgia.

51) When all the colors of the visible spectrum are mixed, what color light is produced?
Answer: White.

52) Which part of the body is affected by the poisonous systemic disease known as *septicemia*?
Answer: The blood.

53) Which American playwright's only real comedy is entitled *Ah, Wilderness!*, a play in which an adolescent, Tommy Miller, has his first experiences in the adult world?
Answer: Eugene O'Neill.

54) Which work by which Alabama author opens with the line, "When he was nearly thirteen, my brother Jem got his arm badly broken at the elbow"?
Answer: *To Kill a Mockingbird* by Harper Lee.

55) In which city in New York was The Declaration of Sentiments demanding equal rights for women penned in 1848?
Answer: Seneca Falls.

56) Identify one of the 2 women who led the Women's Right's Convention in Seneca Falls, New York, on July 19, 1848.
Answer: Lucretia Mott or Elizabeth Cady Stanton.

57) Which Spanish artist painted *Persistence of Memory* in 1932, or what is the more popular name for this painting?
Answer: Salvador Dali or *Soft Watches*.

58) Which French artist is well remembered for his *Nude Descending a Staircase*?
Answer: Marcel Duchamp.

59) Henri Philippe Pétain became the French premier in 1940. After he concluded an armistice with Germany, what name was given

to the fascist-oriented government of unoccupied France in which he became chief-of-state?
Answer: Vichy.

60) Which 2 methods of warfare were prohibited by the Geneva Protocol of 1925?
Answer: Chemical and biological warfare.

61) *Stand and Deliver* is a film about Jaime Escalante, an East Los Angeles barrio high school teacher. What subject does he teach?
Answer: Mathematics.

62) Name the mathematical "theorem" for which the most incorrect proofs have been published. The theorem states, *There exist no positive integers a, b, c, and n such that $a^n + b^n = c^n$, when n is greater than 2.*
Answer: Fermat's last "theorem."

63) In which U.S. state did the severest earthquake ever recorded in North America occur on March 27, 1964, killing 114?
Answer: Alaska (8.5 on the Richter Scale).

64) Identify the Western territory where suffrage was first granted to women in 1869.
Answer: Wyoming.

65) Which region of China is called the "Roof of the World"?
Answer: Tibet.

66) Which city, called "The Rooftop of the World," is the capital of Tibet?
Answer: Lhasa.

67) Which is greatest: the square root of 4/9, 4/9, or 1/2?
Answer: Square root of 4/9.

68) If a piece of wood weighing 12 ounces is found to have a weight of 9 ounces after drying, what was the moisture content of the wood in percent?
Answer: 25%.

69) Name the man who in 1973 became the first black mayor of a large Southern city when he was elected mayor of Atlanta.
Answer: Maynard Jackson.

70) Identify the Secretary of the Treasury under George Washington who proposed an excise tax, one that especially applied to distilled liquors.
Answer: Alexander Hamilton.

71) Name the 4th planet from the sun, also known as "The Red Planet" and named after the Roman god of war.
Answer: Mars.

72) What are the 3 colors of television screen phosphors?
Answer: Red, blue, and green.

73) Which work by John Steinbeck begins with the line, "To the red country and part of the gray country of Oklahoma, the last rains came gently, and they did not cut the scarred earth"?
Answer: *The Grapes of Wrath.*

74) What is the full title of Karel Capek's play *R.U.R.*?
Answer: *Rossum's Universal Robots.*

75) Who was the oldest delegate at the Constitutional Convention and the oldest signer of the U.S. Constitution?
Answer: (81-year-old) Benjamin Franklin (of Pennsylvania).

76) In which city in which state did representatives from 5 states meet in September 1786 and propose that states appoint commissioners to meet in Philadelphia to revise the Articles of Confederation?
Answer: Annapolis, Maryland.

77) Identify the American primitive painter who started painting when she was 76 years old. She painted simple but realistic scenes of rural life such as *Out for the Christmas Trees.*
Answer: Grandma Moses.

78) Which Dutch artist's *Sunflowers* sold for $39.9 million in 1987? This was the highest price ever paid for a work of art at the time.
Answer: Vincent Van Gogh's.

79) Which French leader said, "Du sublime au ridicule il n'y a qu'un pas," or "From the sublime to the ridiculous is but a step"?
Answer: Napoleon.

80) Name any 2 of what are considered the 4 major civilizations of ancient Mesopotamia.
Answer: Sumerian, Assyrian, Babylonian, and Akkadian.

81) Identify the family of singers whose story was portrayed in the 1965 film *The Sound of Music*.
Answer: Von Trapp family.

82) From which country did the von Trapp family escape in 1938?
Answer: Austria.

83) Who was the first English child born in America?
Answer: Virginia Dare.

84) Identify the Ohio college that was the first U.S. college to award degrees to women, doing so in 1841.
Answer: Oberlin College.

85) Although it is not entirely surrounded by land but is connected with both the Caribbean Sea and the Gulf of Venezuela by a short channel, which lake in Venezuela is sometimes considered to be the largest lake in South America?
Answer: Lake Maracaibo.

86) Name the 2 largest French-speaking cities in the world.
Answer: Paris and Montreal.

87) Name the first all-electronic digital computer.
Answer: ENIAC.

88) Name the English mathematician known for his designs of 2 mechanical computing machines, forerunners of the modern computer.
Answer: Charles Babbage.

89) Name the 2 states in which major league baseball teams typically hold spring training.
Answer: Arizona and Florida.

90) Give the names by which the 2 spring training leagues in major league baseball are known.
Answer: Grapefruit League (Florida) and Cactus League (Arizona).

91) The dates 1531, 1607, 1682, 1758, 1835, 1910, and 1985 indicate the appearance of what celestial body approximately every 76 years?
Answer: Halley's comet.

92) Name the Dutch mathematician, physicist, and astronomer who was the first person to study the polarization of light.
Answer: Christian Huygens.

93) René-François-Armand Sully-Prudhomme was the first one to win which literary prize in 1901?
Answer: Nobel Prize in literature.

94) Name the poet who wrote the elegy *Adonais* or the poet whose death was the inspiration for the elegy.
Answer: Percy Bysshe Shelley or John Keats.

95) Give the term for the powers of the national government reasonably suggested by the Constitution.
Answer: Implied powers.

96) Give the term for the powers that belong to the people or to the states, or give the term for the powers that belong to both national and state governments.
Answer: Reserved powers or concurrent powers.

97) What word from Greek mythology means "pertaining to dance"? This word comes from one of the 9 Muses of the arts, the Muse of the dance and of choral song.
Answer: Terpsichorean (from Terpsichore).

98) Identify the ballerina who formed her own company, Ivy House, in London after leaving Russia in 1913. She is famous for "The Dying Swan," a three-minute solo that she frequently performed.
Answer: Anna Pavlova.

99) To which French king is attributed the expression, "L'Etat, c'est moi" (or "I am the state")?
Answer: Louis XIV.

100) Which French king known as "the lost dauphin" was taken from his mother in 1793 at age 8 and kept in prison until he died in 1795?
Answer: Louis XVII.

CHAPTER SIXTEEN

1) Which youth organization was founded by Sir Robert Baden-Powell in 1908?
Answer: Boy Scouts.

2) Identify the American composer of such songs as "White Christmas" and "Oh, How I Hate to Get Up in the Morning." He celebrated his 100th birthday in 1988.
Answer: Irving Berlin.

3) Name the Washington volcano that erupted on May 18, 1980.
Answer: Mount St. Helens.

4) Which pilot in which year made the first solo trans-Atlantic flight from New York to Paris on May 20-21?
Answer: Charles Lindbergh in 1927.

5) In which U.S. city is Lombard Street, the "world's crookedest street"?
Answer: San Francisco.

6) Which bridge designed by John Roebling and built over the East River opened in 1883?
Answer: Brooklyn Bridge.

7) Fermat's theorem starts with the Pythagorean theorem, which is used to determine the hypotenuse of a right triangle. Give the Pythagorean theorem.
Answer: In a right triangle the square of the hypotenuse equals the sum of the squares of the other two sides.

8) The greatest integer function G assigns to each real number X the largest integer not greater than X. To what integer does G assign the number -1.5?
Answer: -2.

9) In which Alabama city is the annual Blue-Gray game held?
Answer: Montgomery.

10) In which city in which state is the Mummers Day Parade held on January 1?
Answer: Philadelphia, Pennsylvania.

11) In electronics, what is the term for an electric current that continually reverses its direction of flow?
Answer: Alternating Current.

12) Which 2 commonly known forces are in effect when a bucket of water is swung in a vertical circle?
Answer: Centrifugal (away from the center) and centripetal (toward the center).

13) Give the French word translated literally as "to God" and meaning "farewell."
Answer: *Adieu.*

14) Give the German word for "a gloomy feeling of anxiety."
Answer: *Angst.*

15) Which U.S. Vice Presidential candidate made a televised speech on September 23, 1952, in defense of a "secret slush fund" in which he mentioned a dog named Checkers and about which he said, "We're gonna (sic) keep it!"?
Answer: Richard Nixon.

16) Identify the first female candidate for the Presidency of the U.S. In 1872, she ran as the candidate of the newly formed Equal Rights Party.
Answer: Victoria Claflin Woodhull.

17) Identify the second of the Biblical Hebrew patriarchs, the son of Abraham and his wife Sarah.
Answer: Isaac.

18) According to the Bible, who were the twin sons of Isaac and his wife Rebecca?
Answer: Esau and Jacob (Genesis 25:21-25).

19) In which year did the Battle of Hastings take place?
Answer: 1066.

20) Name both the Duke of Normandy and the King of England who were the leaders at the Battle of Hastings. The English lost this battle.
Answer: William (I) the Conqueror and King Harold (II).

21) When it opened in 1932, it became the largest indoor theatre in the world. Name this New York City theatre.
Answer: Radio City Music Hall.

22) With which profession are Edward Steichen, Alfred Stieglitz, and Ansel Adams primarily associated?
Answer: Photography.

23) Which U.S. state, long governed by Massachusetts, became the 23rd state as part of the Missouri Compromise in 1820?
Answer: Maine.

24) On which island in which present-day U.S. state was Virginia Dare born in 1587?
Answer: Roanoke Island in North Carolina.

25) In which Asian country does the Grand Canal—one of the oldest and longest on the globe—connect the northern part of the country with the Yangtze River valley?
Answer: China.

26) Identify 2 of the 3 rivers in China in whose basins about 70% of the people, live using just one tenth of the land.
Answer: Yellow (Hwang Ho), Yangtze, and West (Si Kiang).

27) How many yards are equal to 180 inches?
Answer: 5.

28) Change 35% to both a decimal numeral and a fraction in simplest form.
Answer: .35 and 7/20.

29) To which team was Wayne Gretzky of the Edmonton Oilers traded in 1988?
Answer: Los Angeles Kings.

30) Identify the 2 conferences in the National Hockey League.
Answer: (Prince of) Wales Conference and (Clarence) Campbell Conference.

31) Which Russian chemist is considered responsible for devising a Periodic Table of Elements?
Answer: Dmitri Mendeleev (or Mendeleyev).

32) If an element has an octet of electrons in its outer shell, to which family would this element belong?
Answer: Noble Gases (accept inert gases, or Group VIII).

33) According to the saying, what speaks louder than words?
Answer: Actions.

34) Which American writer and mentor to the Lost Generation of writers in Paris after WWI is remembered for writing, "Rose is a rose is a rose is a rose"?
Answer: Gertrude Stein.

35) Identify the former governor of New York who was defeated by Harry Truman in the 1948 Presidential election.
Answer: Thomas E. Dewey.

36) Name the future Chief Justice of the U.S. Supreme Court who was Thomas E. Dewey's running-mate in the 1948 U.S. election.
Answer: Earl Warren.

37) What is the French word for "three"?
Answer: *Trois.*

38) What are the Spanish and German words for "three"?
Answer: *Tres* and *drei*.

39) During which war did the English leader Edward, the "Black Prince," capture France's King John II and his son Philip in the Battle of Poitiers on September 19, 1356?
Answer: Hundred Years War.

40) Which group of religious people in which country were the object of the St. Bartholomew's Day Massacre that began on August 24, 1572?
Answer: Huguenots in France.

41) 40% of what number is 50?
Answer: 125.

42) What is the formula for the volume of a right circular cylinder?
Answer: V = π r squared h (V = pi r² h; where r is the radius of the base, h is the height of the cylinder).

43) Their names are translated into English as "the little girl," "a spotted mare," and "the Mother of Christ." Give the names of these 3 ships of Christopher Columbus on his first voyage to the New World.
Answer: *Niña, Pinta, and Santa María.*

44) Give the month, day, and year when Christopher Columbus is credited with the discovery of the New World.
Answer: October 12, 1492.

45) In which body of water is the island of Sardinia?
Answer: Mediterranean Sea.

46) In which body of water is the island of Hispaniola?
Answer: Caribbean Sea.

47) If a true-false test consists of 3 questions, in how many different ways can they be answered?
Answer: 8.

48) Solve the following proportion: $8/6 = x/27$.
Answer: x = 36.

49) Which art term designates "a large painting done directly on a wall"?
Answer: Mural.

50) Which art term designates "a thin board on which colors are placed and mixed"?
Answer: Palette.

51) Identify the Irish-born British scientist considered the "Founder of Modern Chemistry." He argued that all basic physical properties were due to the motion of atoms, which he termed "corpuscles."
Answer: Robert Boyle.

52) Identify 3 of the 4 basic substances that make up the world according to Empedocles. Boyle showed that these substances are not true elements.
Answer: Air, earth, fire, and water.

53) Who created the characters Frodo and Bilbo Baggins?
Answer: J.R.R. Tolkien.

54) Where do the Hobbits live in J.R.R. Tolkien's fantasies?
Answer: Middle Earth.

55) How many electoral votes are needed to win the U.S. Presidential election?
Answer: 270.

56) Name the 2 states with the most electoral votes.
Answer: California (47) and New York (36).

57) Give the Moslem greeting that is translated in English as "Peace" or "health (be) with you (to you)."
Answer: *Salaam Aleikum.*

58) Name the great Moslem warrior of the 1100s who captured Jerusalem in 1187. The Moslems regarded him as a saintly hero, and even the Christians honored him for his honesty and bravery.
Answer: Saladin (or Sala al din).

59) From which country did Panama separate itself in 1903 to form an independent nation?
Answer: Colombia.

60) Identify the battle during the War of 1812 that marked the first time England had ever surrendered a naval squadron. The battle took place on September 10, 1813.
Answer: Battle of Lake Erie (also called Put-in-Bay).

61) Which element of the halogen group derives its name from the Greek for "stench"? This dark red liquid now obtained from sea water is used in antiknock compounds for gasoline.
Answer: Bromine.

62) Which 3 elements form the basis of all fertilizers in common use?
Answer: Nitrogen, phosphorus, and potassium.

63) Who assassinated Robert Kennedy on June 5, 1968?
Answer: Sirhan Sirhan.

64) Give the Supreme Court decision of June 1966 that holds that the Fifth Amendment "requires warnings before valid statements can be taken by police."
Answer: Miranda Decision.

65) In which European capital would you watch the Spanish Riding School perform in its home arena?
Answer: Vienna (Austria).

66) Name 2 of the 3 largest Italian volcanoes.
Answer: Etna (Aetna), Vesuvius, and Stromboli.

67) Change 16 2/3% to a fraction in simplest form.
Answer: 1/6.

68) What is 25% of 3 hours and 20 minutes?
Answer: 5/6 of an hour or 50 minutes.

69) Name the 8th nation and the first one in the Middle East to launch a satellite into orbit. It did so in 1988.
Answer: Israel.

70) In which English city did Pilgrim's Way, a shrine to the tales written by Geoffrey Chaucer, open in 1988?
Answer: Canterbury.

71) What is the property of a substance that determines the speed of light in that medium?
Answer: Index of refraction (or optical density).

72) Identify the pendulum that can demonstrate the rotation of the earth. This pendulum, named after its 1851 inventor, is dependent upon the principle of Newton's first law of motion.
Answer: Foucault pendulum.

73) In which Shakespearean play do the following characters appear: Claudius, Polonius, and Ophelia?
Answer: *Hamlet.*

74) In which Shakespearean play do the following characters appear: Malvolio, Orsino, and Olivia?
Answer: *Twelfth Night, or What You Will.*

75) Which Kansas city completes the name of the landmark 1954 *Brown v. The Board of Education of* _________ decision that segregation in public schools was not constitutional?
Answer: Topeka.

76) Name the 2 youngest U.S. Presidents. One became President after the death of William McKinley, and the other was elected in 1960.
Answer: Teddy Roosevelt and John Kennedy.

77) What feast day commemorates the visit of the Magi, or Three Wise Men, to the infant Jesus (Matthew 2:1-16)?
Answer: Feast of the Epiphany (January 6).

78) According to Psalms 111:10, what is the beginning of wisdom?
Answer: "The fear of the Lord."

79) Which name meaning "the exalted" was given to Gaius Julius Caesar Octavianus (Octavian) when he became the first Roman emperor in 27 B.C.?
Answer: Augustus.

80) Name 2 of the 4 emperors who succeeded Augustus.
Answer: Tiberius, Caligula, Claudius, and Nero.

81) Name either the U.S. Air Force or the U.S. Navy flying team.
Answer: Thunderbirds or Blue Angels.

82) Give the phrase for "all the water or oceans of the world." This phrase has no literal meaning as it preceded an exact knowledge of the number of the world's bodies of water?
Answer: Seven seas.

83) Washington Irving described this President's wife as "fine and portly" with "a smile and a pleasant word for everybody," then added, "as to Jeemy . . . ah! poor Jeemy!—He is but a withered little apple-John." Name him.
Answer: James Madison.

84) Which college did James Madison attend? When he was there, it was known as the College of New Jersey.
Answer: Princeton University.

85) Identify the elevated part of Athens, Greece, whose name in translation means "high city."
Answer: Acropolis.

86) Identify the most important temple of Athena. It was erected between 447 and 432 B.C. on the Acropolis.
Answer: Parthenon.

87) Identify the repetend in the decimal for 3/11.
Answer: 27.

88) What is the number named by the square of the result of squaring 3?
Answer: 81.

89) In which state is the Little League Baseball World Series annually played in the town of Williamsport?
Answer: Pennsylvania.

90) Which National League manager for which team was suspended from baseball in 1989 for betting on major league baseball games? IIe allegedly bet on his own team.
Answer: Pete Rose of the Cincinnati Reds.

91) An atom is found to have an atomic number of 11 and a mass number of 23. How many neutrons does the atom have?
Answer: 12.

92) How many molecules are contained in 1 mole of water?
Answer: 6.02×10^{23} molecules (or 6.022×10^{23} or 6.022045×10^{23}).

93) Who is the author of *The White Company*, a historical novel; "The Red-Headed League," a short story; and *A Study in Scarlet*, a detective novel?
Answer: Sir Arthur Conan Doyle.

94) Name 2 of Aristophanes' 3 extant comedies, each with an animal in the title and the same number of letters.
Answer: *The Frogs*, *The Birds*, and *The Wasps*.

95) Name the government position held by all of the following women: Margaret Hance, Kathy Whitmire, Dianne Feinstein,

and Jane Byrne.
Answer: Mayor of a U.S. city (Phoenix, Houston, San Francisco, and Chicago respectively).

96) Name 2 of the 3 U.S. Presidents from Tennessee, none of whom was born in the state.
Answer: Andrew Jackson, James Polk, and Andrew Johnson.

97) According to Greek mythology, who was the Muse of history?
Answer: Clio.

98) Name 2 of the 3 goddesses at the wedding of Peleus and Thetis into whose midst Eris, the Greek goddess of Discord, threw a golden apple on which was inscribed "the fairest woman."
Answer: Hera, Athena, and Aphrodite.

99) Which word, derived from the Greek for "to burn whole," designates the systematic destruction of over 6 million European Jews by the Nazis during WWII and is recalled in the TV film *Escape From Sobibor?*
Answer: Holocaust.

100) A Hungarian government newspaper broke official silence in 1987 on the disappearance of which Swedish diplomat who vanished after saving the lives of many Hungarian Jews during WWII? This diplomat allegedly died in 1947 in Moscow's Lubyanka Prison as a victim of Josef Stalin's personality cult.
Answer: Raoul Wallenberg.

CHAPTER SEVENTEEN

1) In which country is Balmoral Castle, the summer residence of Queen Elizabeth II?
Answer: Scotland.

2) Who are the parents of Princess Beatrice of York, born at 8 minutes after 8:00 p.m. on August 8, 1988?
Answer: Prince Andrew and Duchess Sarah.

3) Name the Sioux Indian portrayed in a gigantic unfinished sculpture in the Black Hills of South Dakota started by Korczak Ziolkowski.
Answer: Crazy Horse.

4) Which American Army officer who rose to the rank of brigadier general was court-martialed for insubordination in September 1925?
Answer: William "Billy" Mitchell.

5) In which country do the Ganges and the Brahmaputra/Jamuna, 2 of the world's greatest rivers, frequently overflow to cause death and destruction?
Answer: Bangladesh.

6) On which body of water is Bangladesh located?
Answer: Bay of Bengal.

7) Evaluate 2 cubed times 3 squared.
Answer: 72.

8) Solve the following equation: of $2y - 7 = -29$ (*two y minus seven equals negative twenty-nine*).
Answer: $y = -11$ (*y equals negative eleven*).

9) Who was the first American to win the Tour de France?
Answer: Greg LeMond.

10) Who became the manager of the Cleveland Indians in 1975, as the first black manager in major league baseball?
Answer: Frank Robinson.

11) Name the delicate instrument used to detect and measure the strength of an electric current.
Answer: Galvanometer (accept ammeter).

12) Identify the British scientist and cousin of Charles Darwin who was the first to call the science of human breeding *eugenics*.
Answer: Sir Francis Galton.

13) Identify the English author of *The War of the Worlds*.
Answer: H.G. Wells.

14) Who is the American author of *Eclectic Readers*?
Answer: William H. McGuffey.

15) Identify the Missouri senator who acknowledged receiving electric shock therapy to combat mental illness and who was the vice presidential pick of Democratic presidential candidate George McGovern in 1972.
Answer: Thomas Eagleton.

16) Identify the Republican running mates in the 1960 Presidential election who were defeated by John F. Kennedy and Lyndon Johnson.
Answer: Richard Nixon and Henry Cabot Lodge.

17) On which Biblical mount did Moses receive the Ten Commandments?
Answer: Mount Sinai.

18) On which Biblical mount did Moses view the Promised Land?
Answer: Mount Pisgah (accept its highest peak, Mount Nebo).

19) Which war began when an invasion took place on June 25, 1950? It ended when an armistice was signed on July 27, 1953, at Panmunjom.
Answer: Korean War.

20) Which king in which year granted many rights to English aristocrats in a document sealed in a meadow called Runnymede on June 15?
Answer: King John in 1215.

21) Of which union did Owen Bieber become the president, a union known by the initials UAW?
Answer: United Auto Workers.

22) The Liberty Bell suffered a crack on July 8, 1835, while it was tolling for the death of which U.S. Supreme Court Chief Justice?
Answer: John Marshall.

23) Name the American Revolutionary War hero who served as a rear admiral in the Black Sea fleet for Empress Catherine II of Russia from 1788-1789.
Answer: John Paul Jones.

24) Give the surname of the U.S. couple executed for espionage on June 19, 1953.
Answer: (Julius and Ethel) Rosenberg.

25) In which U.S. state is Mount Rushmore?
Answer: South Dakota.

26) Name the 3 states in which the Yellowstone National Park is located.
Answer: Wyoming, Montana, and Idaho.

27) What is the value of 2 to the 5th power?
Answer: 32.

28) Express the rational number 0.4375 as a fraction in reduced form.
Answer: 7/16.

29) In which Central American country was Daniel Ortega elected president in 1984?
Answer: Nicaragua.

30) Name any 2 of the 4 nations involved in the Contadora Group or Process. This group's philosophical approach favors a peaceful negotiation to settle political disputes in Central America.
Answer: Colombia, Venezuela, Panama, and Mexico.

31) Identify the unit used for measuring wavelengths of light, and named after a Swedish physicist. It is equal to one ten-millionth of a millimeter.
Answer: Angstrom.

32) Identify the SI unit used to measure the frequency of light waves, and named after a German physicist. It is equivalent to one cycle per second.
Answer: Hertz.

33) In Rudyard Kipling's *The Ballad of East and West*, which word completes the line, "Oh, East is East, and West is West, and never the _________ shall meet"?
Answer: "twain."

34) In which work by which author is Brobdingnag a region where everything is of tremendous size?
Answer: *Gulliver's Travels* by Jonathan Swift.

35) Identify the American cartoonist who popularized the Democratic donkey, the Republican elephant, and the Tammany tiger.
Answer: Thomas Nast.

36) Identify the commission whose report released on September 27, 1964, concluded that Lee Harvey Oswald "acted alone" in killing President Kennedy.
Answer: Warren Commission.

37) Name the wife of the mythological Odysseus.
Answer: Penelope.

38) Give the name of the ivory statue of a maiden carved by Pygmalion, a sculptor and king of Epirus. This statue was brought to life by Aphrodite.
Answer: Galatea.

39) On which Japanese city on August 9, 1945, was a plutonium bomb nicknamed "Fat Man" dropped by the American bomber *Bock's Car*?
Answer: Nagasaki.

40) Which American bomber dropped the first atomic bomb on which Japanese city on August 6, 1945?
Answer: *Enola Gay* on Hiroshima.

41) What is the plural of the geometrical name for a figure that is the set of all points and only those points that satisfy one or more given conditions?
Answer: Loci.

42) What is the locus of points in a given plane 10 cm from a given line in that plane?
Answer: 2 lines (the 2 lines are parallel to the given line).

43) In which month, day, and year did the colonists officially adopt the Declaration of Independence and form the United States of America?
Answer: July 4, 1776.

44) Give the beginning and ending years of the U.S. Civil War.
Answer: 1861-1865.

45) Which name belongs to a U.S. capital, a university in New York, a major U.S. river, and a U.S. space shuttle?
Answer: Columbia.

46) Which 2 countries are connected by the Khyber Pass?
Answer: Afghanistan and Pakistan.

47) If $f(x)$ (*read as f of x*) represents a function, what term is used to describe the set of all admissible values of x?
Answer: Domain.

48) Given the rational function $f(x) = x/(x^2 - 5x + 6)$ [*read as f of x equals x divided by the quantity x squared minus 5x plus 6*], which real numbers are *not* permitted in the domain of $f(x)$?
Answer: 2 and 3.

49) In which museum is the celebrated larger-than-life Greek marble statue entitled *Victory of Samothrace*?
Answer: Louvre (in Paris).

50) The statue *Victory of Samothrace* represents the Greek goddess of Victory alighting on the bows of a galley. Name this goddess.
Answer: Nike.

51) Identify either of the following state flowers from the clues. You'd need an elephant to remember Alaska's state flower, or if you'd hang around at Christmas, you'd know the state flower of Oklahoma.
Answer: Forget-me-not, or mistletoe.

52) Why do astronomers classify Sirius, the Dog Star, as a *binary star* system?
Answer: Because it has a companion star.

53) Give the word derived from a Manhattan street pattern and defined as "any situation in which nothing, especially traffic, can move in any direction."
Answer: Gridlock.

54) Give the term defined in Webster's 1988 *New World Dictionary* as "a high-yield speculative bond often issued to finance the take-over of a corporation."
Answer: Junk bond.

55) Which word ending in *-archy* means "absence of any form of political authority"?
Answer: Anarchy.

56) Name 3 of the 4 U.S. states which are still officially designated as "Commonwealths."
Answer: Kentucky, Massachusetts, Pennsylvania, and Virginia.

57) Give the name of the religious cult, originally Jamaican in origin, that regards Africa as the Promised Land to which all true believers will someday return.
Answer: Rastafarianism.

58) Name the former emperor of Ethiopia who is considered to be the messiah of Rastafarianism.
Answer: Haile Selassie (I).

59) Identify the 19th century Italian military hero who fought to unite Italy into a single kingdom. He worked as a candlemaker in New York for a while before returning to Italy in 1854.
Answer: Giuseppe Garibaldi.

60) Identify the famous volunteer troops of Giuseppe Garibaldi with whose help he conquered the Kingdom of the Two Sicilies for the Kingdom of Italy.
Answer: Red Shirts.

61) Identify the hard black stone made up of magnetite that was first used as a magnet in compasses.
Answer: Lodestone (or loadstone).

62) Identify the kind of silt that forms a fertile topsoil in some parts of the world. This loose surface sediment is derived from the German word for "loose."
Answer: Loess.

63) Against which U.S. President were charges made by his opponents that he had fathered several children by Sally Hemings, a slave woman?
Answer: Thomas Jefferson.

64) At which site in which territory did General Custer make his last stand on June 25-26, 1876?
Answer: Little Bighorn in Montana.

65) In which swamp does Walt Kelly's comic strip character Pogo Possum make his home?
Answer: Okefenokee Swamp.

66) In which 2 states is the Okefenokee Swamp?
Answer: Georgia and Florida.

67) If each edge of a cube is tripled, by how much will the volume of the cube increase?
Answer: By 27 times.

68) What conic section is the result of graphing the relationship $x^2 + 4y^2 = 25$ (*x squared plus four y squared equals twenty-five*)?
Answer: Ellipse.

69) Identify the female athlete who set the world record in 1988 in the 100-meter dash with a 10.49 seconds, bettering the old 10.76.
Answer: Florence Griffith Joyner.

70) In which race in 1988 did Butch Reynolds smash a 20-year-old world record with a clocking of 43.29 seconds, bettering Lee Evans' record of 43.86 set in October 1968 at the Olympic Games in Mexico?
Answer: 400 meters.

71) What date is the first day of summer in the Northern Hemisphere?
Answer: June 20 (or 21 or 22).

72) Which planet did Adams and Le Verrier predict by means of mathematics before it was seen through a telescope? It is named after the Roman god of the sea.
Answer: Neptune.

73) Identify the 1951 Nikos Kazantzakis novel on which Martin Scorsese based his 1988 film that raised a storm of protest from the Christian community.
Answer: *The Last Temptation of Christ*.

74) In which work by which author is Molly Bloom a fictional character?
Answer: *Ulysses* by James Joyce.

75) Identify the resolution approved on August 7, 1964, which gave President Johnson the authority to "take all necessary measures to repel any armed attack against the forces of the U.S....and to assist any member of the Southeast Asia Collective Defense Treaty."
Answer: Gulf of Tonkin Resolution.

76) Which country suffered a humiliating defeat in 1954 at Dien Bien Phu in Vietnam?
Answer: France.

77) Identify the organization founded in 1540 by Saint Ignatius Loyola and often called the "Pope's Light Cavalry."
Answer: Jesuits (or the Society of Jesus).

78) Identify the Christian leader of the 4th and 5th century who wrote *The City of God*.
Answer: Saint Augustine.

79) Which explorer became, on September 25, 1513, the first European to see the eastern shore of the Pacific Ocean?
Answer: Vasco Núñez de Balboa.

80) Balboa called the Pacific Ocean the South Sea. Identify the Portuguese explorer who in 1520 named the ocean the Pacific, which means "peaceful," because it seemed calmer than the Atlantic.
Answer: Ferdinand Magellan.

81) Haboobs exist in northern Africa. Are they hoods for Berber tribesmen, thick dust storms, oases, or desert nomads?
Answer: Thick dust (or sand) storms.

82) If you were in a building and someone defenestrated you, what happened to you?
Answer: You were thrown out a window.

83) Which U.S. President upon completing his first cup of Maxwell House coffee said that it was "good to the last drop"?
Answer: Theodore Roosevelt.

84) What was the name of William Lloyd Garrison's abolitionist newspaper?
Answer: *The Liberator*.

85) What is the capital of Hungary?
Answer: Budapest.

86) Name 2 of the 3 European capitals that begin with the letter "V." They are the capitals of Liechtenstein, Malta, and Austria.
Answer: Vaduz (Liechtenstein); Valletta (Malta); and Vienna (Austria)—some but not most sources list Vatican City as the capital of Vatican City.

87) In the arithmetic progression whose first term is 15 and whose common difference is 4, what is the 3rd term?
Answer: 23.

88) What is the derivative of 3 times x to the 9th power minus 3 times x to the 5th power?
Answer: $27x$ to the 8th power minus $15x$ to the 4th power.

89) On which day is International Labor Day celebrated?
Answer: May 1.

90) In which Scandinavian country was Prime Minister Olof Palme shot to death by an assassin on February 28, 1986?
Answer: Sweden.

91) What are the 2 parts of the scientific name of an organism?
Answer: Genus and species.

92) You're a king—a chess king, to be exact—and you're standing on the periodic table, squarely on Chlorine. Name any 2 of the 8 elements to which you can legally move.
Answer: Fluorine (9), neon (10), argon (18), krypton (36), bromine (35), selenium (34), sulfur (16), oxygen (8). [chlorine is 17].

93) Name the American creator and author of *The Bobbsey Twins, Nancy Drew*, and *The Hardy Boys*.
Answer: Edward L. Stratemeyer (accept Harriet Stratemeyer Adams).

94) Name the official poet of Victorian England who served as Poet Laureate from 1850-1892 and is called "The Bard of Arthurian Romance."
Answer: Alfred Lord Tennyson.

95) Identify the Presidential candidate who was depicted as a "Baboon" before the election of 1864.
Answer: Abraham Lincoln.

96) Give the month, day, and year Pearl Harbor was struck by the Japanese.
Answer: December 7, 1941.

97) What is the name of the chemical element having as its symbol *As*? It occurs in nature in dull gray flakes and is a deadly poison used in insecticides.
Answer: Arsenic.

98) Identify the Egyptian some consider the first scientist and physician. He was the architect of the step-pyramid at the village of Saqqarah, and he was worshipped for his healing powers by the Egyptians while the Greeks identified him with Asclepius, their own god of healing.
Answer: Imhotep.

99) Identify the Roman general and statesman who formed the First Triumvirate with Julius Caesar and Marcus Crassus.
Answer: Pompey (the Great).

100) In 49 B.C., Julius Caesar marched with his 5,000 troops against Pompey. What is the ancient name of the river or small stream in northern Italy that he crossed, a decision that was tantamount to declaring war?
Answer: Rubicon.

CHAPTER EIGHTEEN

1) Identify the solemn promise of loyalty to the U.S. attributed to Francis Bellamy.
   Answer: Pledge of Allegiance.

2) What is the Arabic title used to designate a respected man or the chief of a family, tribe, or village? This title is used sometimes to refer to a religious leader.
   Answer: Sheik (or sheikh).

3) In the year that Eli Whitney filed a patent claim for his cotton gin, Marie Antoinette and Louis XVI were executed. What was the year?
   Answer: 1793.

4) Which U.S. President was assassinated by which person in a train station in Washington, D.C. on July 2, 1881?
   Answer: James Garfield by Charles Guiteau.

5) In which Georgia city is the Jimmy Carter National Historic Site?
   Answer: Plains.

6) In which city in which country was the World's Fair known as Expo 67 held? This Fair's theme was "Man and His World."
   Answer: Montreal, Canada (in 1967).

7) Solve for x in the equation $4x + 6 = 2x + 8$.
   Answer: 1.

8) Give the x-intercept of the graph determined by the line $y = x$.
   Answer: 0.

9) Give the name of the space shuttle that successfully carried the American flag back into orbit in 1988 after a 32-month absence.
   Answer: *Discovery.*

10) From which site in which U.S. state did *Discovery* blast off in 1988?
Answer: Cape Canaveral, Florida.

11) Which part of the human body, often described as vermiform, is considered to be vestigial?
Answer: Appendix (the vermiform appendix).

12) What is the ratio of the genes in a single zygote to those in a single gamete of a particular species?
Answer: 2 to 1.

13) What is the name of Aldous Huxley's satirical novel of 1932 whose title comes from William Shakespeare's comedy *The Tempest*?
Answer: *Brave New World.*

14) Which 3 words complete the passage in *Leviathan* in which Thomas Hobbes describes the existence of men without an all-powerful leader to direct them as " solitary, poor, _________, _________, and _________ "?
Answer: "nasty, brutish, and short."

15) Name the U.S. President who was the last Civil War veteran to achieve the presidency. His Vice President was Theodore Roosevelt.
Answer: William McKinley.

16) Identify the 1984 Democratic vice presidential candidate to Walter Mondale, who embarrassed him by stories questioning her finances.
Answer: Geraldine Ferraro.

17) What is the name of a northern constellation between Cygnus and Aquarius, a name derived from that of the mythological horse created from the blood or neck of Medusa?
Answer: Pegasus.

18) The ruler Dionysius arranged at a feast for a flatterer to sit under a weapon suspended by a single thread to demonstrate the uncertainty of human happiness. What phrase derived from this myth is used today to designate "any impending danger"?
Answer: Sword of Damocles.

19) Columbus landed on Guanahani or Samana Cay in the Bahamas on October 12, 1492. What did he name this island?
Answer: San Salvador.

20) What is the present day name of the island whose climate and trees reminded Columbus so much of Spain that he named it *La Isla Española*, the Spanish Island?
Answer: Hispaniola.

21) Give the name for the 2nd full moon of the month, one that appeared in July 1985, in May 1988, and again in December 1990.
Answer: Blue moon.

22) Identify the English astronomer and mathematician who was the first to calculate the orbit of a comet named for him.
Answer: Edmund Halley.

23) Which Civil War battle in Maryland in 1862 served as background for these lines from John Greenleaf Whittier: " 'Shoot, if you must, this old gray head / But spare your country's flag,' she said"?
Answer: Antietam, or Sharpsburg.

24) Which mortally wounded American naval officer aboard the *Chesapeake* in a naval duel with the H.M.S. *Shannon* off the coast of Canada, on June 1, 1813, uttered his famous last words, "Don't give up the ship"?
Answer: Captain James Lawrence.

25) What is the word for the "the area of the earth's surface directly above the focus of an earthquake"?
Answer: Epicenter.

26) What name is given to the theory that the earth's crust consists of about 20 rigid plates that move slowly past one another?
Answer: Plate tectonics.

27) In which quadrant of a Cartesian coordinate system would you find the point with the ordered pair (7, − 3)?
Answer: Quadrant IV.

28) Find the principal square root of 9 and multiply it by 9 times the principal square root of 9.
Answer: 81.

29) In which country did ethnic and economic protests create disturbances in 1988 not only in the capital of Belgrade but also in some of the 6 republics and 2 provinces?
Answer: Yugoslavia.

30) Name 2 of the 6 republics of Yugoslavia.
Answer: Bosnia and Hercegovina, Croatia, Macedonia, Montenegro, Serbia, and Slovenia.

31) Name the Australian nurse who developed a method of treating poliomyelitis.
Answer: (Sister) Elizabeth Kenny.

32) Name the bicycle-making brothers who demonstrated America's first successful gasoline-powered automobile in Massachusetts in 1893.
Answer: Charles and Frank Duryea.

33) What name is given to any prose narrative about legendary heroes written in Iceland between the 1100s and the 1300s?
Answer: Saga.

34) Which set of classics has become famous as the "five-foot shelf of books," or at which American university did the president, Charles William Eliot, edit these works?
Answer: Harvard Classics, or Harvard University.

35) Which amendment provides that when the Vice Presidency is vacant, the President shall nominate a replacement, and that both houses of Congress by majority vote must approve the nominee?
Answer: 25th Amendment.

36) About whom was he speaking and after the assassination of which President did Mark Hanna say, "Now look, that damned cowboy is President of the United States"?
Answer: Theodore Roosevelt after William McKinley was assassinated (1901).

37) According to the Bible (Genesis 4:16), to which country did Cain journey after killing Abel?
Answer: Land of Nod (to the east of Eden).

38) Which U.S. President is associated with the passage from Isaiah 1:18, "Come now, let us reason together"?
Answer: Lyndon B. Johnson.

39) Give the beginning and ending years of WWI.
Answer: 1914-1918.

40) Give the beginning and ending years of WWII.
Answer: 1939-1945.

41) What is the length of the hypotenuse of a right triangle whose legs are 30 and 40?
Answer: 50.

42) What are the numerical values of both the sine and cosine of a 60° angle?
Answer: Sin 60° = 3/2; cos 60° = 1/2.

43) Which American humorist and social critic said, "All politics is applesauce"?
Answer: Will Rogers.

44) Which American abolitionist said, "I am in earnest—I will not equivocate—I will not excuse—I will not retreat a single inch—AND I WILL BE HEARD?
Answer: William Lloyd Garrison.

45) Identify the Soviet town that was razed in 1988 because it was not fit for human habitation. It was the site of the world's worst nuclear accident.
Answer: Chernobyl.

46) Between which 2 continents is the Drake Passage? This strait is located between Cape Horn and the South Shetland Islands.
Answer: South America and Antarctica.

47) Give the number of noncollinear points needed to determine a plane.
Answer: 3.

48) What are the real roots of the equation $3x^2 - 27 = 0$ (three x squared minus twenty-seven equals zero)?
Answer: 3 and –3.

49) The beautiful Greek statue *Winged Victory* now in the Louvre was found on the island of Samothrace. In which sea is Samothrace?
Answer: Aegean Sea.

50) The Greek statue *Winged Victory* was erected by the Greeks to honor Nike, goddess of victory. Name the 2 parts of this statue which are missing.
Answer: Head and arms.

51) Identify the Russian physiologist famous for developing the concept of the conditioned reflex.
Answer: Ivan Pavlov.

52) Name the English physicist and chemist who discovered the properties of hydrogen and identified it as an element, calling it "inflammable air."
Answer: Henry Cavendish.

53) In which Shakespearean play do the following characters appear: Shylock, Portia, and Antonio?
Answer: *The Merchant of Venice.*

54) In which Shakespearean play do the following characters appear: Duncan, Malcolm, and Banquo?
Answer: *Macbeth.*

55) How often are elections held for the U.S. House of Representatives?
Answer: Every 2 years.

56) Give 2 of the 3 requirements to become a member of the U.S. House of Representatives.
Answer: 25 years of age, a citizen of the U.S. for 7 years, and an inhabitant of that state when elected.

57) Name the goddess of warfare and wisdom in Greek mythology. She was also the patron goddess of Athens.
Answer: Athena (or Pallas Athena).

58) Identify the group of ancient sculptures taken from the Acropolis to England by Thomas Bruce, 7th Earl of Elgin.
Answer: Elgin Marbles (taken about 1806).

59) If the U.S. ceases to make conquests in space, with which country noted for its daring explorers of the 1400s and 1500s will it be compared? After the Spanish takeover in 1580, this country lost most of its colonial holdings.
Answer: Portugal.

60) Identify the imaginary line drawn by Pope Alexander VI to settle land rights in 1493. He hoped it would prevent disputes between Spain and Portugal in Asia and the Americas.
Answer: Line of Demarcation.

61) Identify the island off the west coast of Africa on which Sir Edmund Halley catalogued from 1676 to 1678 the positions of about 350 Southern Hemisphere stars. Napoleon died on this island in 1821.
Answer: Saint Helena.

62) Identify both the year of birth and the year of death of Mark Twain. He was born the year the comet Halley appeared in the 19th century and died in the year it reappeared in the 20th century.
Answer: 1835-1910.

63) Identify the famous Civil War photographer who also published a volume of portraits in 1850 entitled *A Gallery of Illustrious Americans*.
Answer: Mathew Brady.

64) At which site in which state did the first atomic bomb explosion occur on July 16, 1945?
Answer: Trinity Site (Alamagordo Air Base) in New Mexico.

65) Between which states is the Chesapeake Bay?
Answer: Maryland and Virginia.

66) Identify the deepest inland lake in the U.S. and the state in which it is located. Scientists used a one-person submersible craft to scan the lake's bottom in 1988.
Answer: Crater Lake in Oregon.

67) What is the total surface area of a cube whose edge measures 8 cm?
Answer: 384 square cm.

68) What is the probability of getting a sum of 9 on a single toss of a pair of dice?
Answer: 4 out of 36 or 1 out of 9.

69) Which country's plane carrying 290 passengers was accidentally shot down over the Persian Gulf on July 3, 1988, by the USS *Vincennes*?
Answer: Iran's.

70) In which South American country did the opponents achieve a ballot-box victory over the military rule of President Augusto Pinochet in 1988?
Answer: Chile (55% to 43%).

71) Which letter of the Greek alphabet is used in astronomy to designate the brightest star in a constellation?
Answer: Alpha.

72) Which word meaning "humpbacked" refers to the phase of the moon when it is more than half full but less than full?
Answer: Gibbous.

73) Identify the linen-weaver in a George Eliot novel who, driven out of a town on a false theft charge, takes refuge in Raveloe.
Answer: Silas Marner.

74) Identify the little foundling child who restores Silas Marner to happiness.
Answer: Eppie.

75) Richard Nixon's Vice President, Spiro Agnew, resigned after pleading no-contest to bribery and kick-back charges while he was a state official. Of which state was he the governor?
Answer: Maryland.

76) Identify either of the 2 Richard Nixon appointees to the U.S. Supreme Court who were rejected by the Senate in 1969 and 1970.
Answer: Clement Haynsworth or G. Harrold Carswell.

77) Name the first book of both the Old and the New Testament.
Answer: Genesis and Matthew.

78) Name 2 of the 3 saints whose voices Joan of Arc said she heard.
Answer: St. Michael, St. Margaret, and St. Catherine.

79) In which city in which country was a wall erected in 1961 to close the border between East and West?
Answer: East Berlin in East Germany.

80) Which opposition leader in which country was assassinated at the Manila Airport in 1983 when he returned home?
Answer: Benigno Aquino in the Philippines.

81) Which sign of the Zodiac is associated with the date December 25?
Answer: Capricorn.

82) What are the signs of the Zodiac before and after Capricorn?
Answer: Sagittarius and Aquarius.

83) Which American explorer in the *Josephine Ford* in 1926 and in the *Floyd Bennett* in 1929 was the first to fly over the North and the South Poles?
Answer: Richard Byrd.

84) Which naval captain aboard the *Columbia* departed Boston on September 30, 1787, to become the first to circumnavigate the globe on an American ship?
Answer: Captain Robert Gray.

85) In geology, what name is given to the ruptures that occur when the force on the rigid plates in the earth's crust becomes too great?
Answer: Faults.

86) Name the 750-mile fracture in the earth's crust which traverses the length of California.
Answer: San Andreas Fault.

87) By what common graph is the following known: $y = 3$?
Answer: A straight line.

88) By what common graph is the following known: $x^2 + 2y^2 = 1$
(x squared plus two y squared equals one)?
Answer: Ellipse.

89) In how many different fields are Nobel Prizes awarded?
Answer: 6.

90) Which Nobel Prize was awarded for the first time in 1969?
Answer: Economics.

91) In which month on which date in which year did 2 U.S. astronauts become the first humans to land on the moon?
Answer: July 20, 1969.

92) Identify the spacecraft launched from Florida on March 2, 1972.
It departed from the solar system on June 13, 1983, and is now
searching for a Planet X beyond Pluto. It is the first man-made
object to escape the solar system.
Answer: *Pioneer 10*.

93) Identify the western novelist who died in 1988 at age 80. He is
the author of *Hondo, How the West Was Won*, and *Lonigan*.
Answer: Louis L'Amour.

94) In which story by which writer do Bill Driscol and Sam kidnap
a mischievous freckle-faced brat whom they can't get rid of?
Answer: "The Ransom of Red Chief" by O. Henry.

95) Who presides at a Senate impeachment when the U.S. President
is on trial?
Answer: Chief Justice of the Supreme Court.

96) How many members present must concur to convict the President on impeachment charges?
Answer: Two-thirds.

97) In which Tchaikovsky ballet are Princess Aurora, the wicked
fairy, and Prince Florimund?
Answer: *Sleeping Beauty*.

98) In which Tchaikovsky ballet are Prince Siegfried, the evil
magician, Odette, and Odile?
Answer: *Swan Lake*.

99) In which country does the leader sit on the Chrysanthemum Throne?
Answer: Japan.

100) In which country did a 20th century leader sit on the Peacock Throne?
Answer: Iran.

CHAPTER NINETEEN

1) On which day is Labor Day celebrated in the U.S.?
   Answer: First Monday in September.

2) Identify the author of *The Cardinal of the Kremlin*, *Patriot Games*, *Red Storm Rising*, and *Hunt for Red October*.
   Answer: Tom Clancy.

3) Which city did British forces invade and burn on August 24-25, 1814?
   Answer: Washington, D.C.

4) Identify the shoemaker and the fish peddler electrocuted in August 1927 for killing 2 men in a payroll robbery in Massachusetts.
   Answer: Sacco and Vanzetti.

5) Which state's capitol is a replica of the U.S. Capitol, or in which city, also known as the "City of Three Capitols," is it located?
   Answer: Arkansas, or Little Rock.

6) Which U.S. capital was known in the 1800s as the last point on the Pony Express Line?
   Answer: Sacramento (California).

7) By how many degrees Celsius do the boiling point and freezing points of water differ?
   Answer: 100.

8) How many 4-letter permutations can be made from the letters of the word WORK?
   Answer: 24.

9) Which Boston Red Sox player became the first major league player in this century to get 200 hits in 6 consecutive seasons?
   Answer: Wade Boggs.

10) Who became the first man to win 4 Olympic gold medals in diving when he won in both the springboard and platform in the 1988 Olympics?
Answer: Greg Louganis (Pat McCormick won both events in the 1952 and 1956 Games).

11) Identify the biological science that deals with the nature, function, and diseases of the blood.
Answer: Hematology.

12) Identify the order of insects called *true bugs*.
Answer: Hemiptera.

13) Who wrote in *Sonnet 18*, "Shall I compare thee to a summer's day? / Thou art more lovely and more temperate"?
Answer: William Shakespeare.

14) What Shakespearean character said, "I am not only witty in myself, but the cause that wit is in other men"?
Answer: Falstaff.

15) Identify the Maryland-born last surviving signer of the Declaration of Independence, who died November 14, 1832.
Answer: Charles Carroll (of Carrollton).

16) Identify the Secretary of the Interior in the Reagan administration who said in 1983, "We have every kind of mixture you can have. I have a black, a woman, two Jews and a cripple."
Answer: James Watt.

17) On which day in August is the Assumption of the Virgin Mary?
Answer: The 15th.

18) On which day in December is the Feast of the Immaculate Conception?
Answer: The 8th.

19) Which country was once known as the "Hermit Kingdom"?
Answer: Korea.

20) What name was given to the reign of Emperor Hirohito begun in 1926, a name meaning "Enlightened Peace"?
Answer: Showa.

21) Name the French leader whose remains are in a 14 1/2 foot high block of granite in Paris' *Eglise du Dome*, or Church of the Dome. This leader was known as the "Little Corporal."
Answer: Napoleon (I).

22) Which Spanish writer was nicknamed "Maimed (Crippled) of Lepanto" after he was wounded in the chest and left hand at the Battle of Lepanto in 1571?
Answer: Miguel de Cervantes ("*Manco de Lepanto*"; *Manco* is literally "one-armed").

23) Which day of WWII is called "The Longest Day"?
Answer: June 6, 1944 (D-Day, the day of the Allied invasion of Normandy).

24) Identify the New York State Supreme Court judge who disappeared forever in August 1930.
Answer: Judge Joseph Force Crater.

25) In which California city did a major earthquake occur in 1906 with the loss of about 500 lives?
Answer: San Francisco.

26) What name is given to the circum-Pacific belt, along which more than three-fourths of the world's earthquakes occur?
Answer: Ring of Fire.

27) What is the numerical value of 1 factorial divided by 0 factorial?
Answer: 1.

28) What unit fraction is roughly equivalent to .1429?
Answer: 1/7.

29) Give the full name of the ACLU, a nonpartisan organization devoted to defending the rights and freedoms of people in the U.S.
Answer: American Civil Liberties Union.

30) Give the full name of RICO, an act that allows the government to freeze assets suspected of being illegally acquired.
Answer: Racketeer Influenced and Corrupt Organizations Act.

31) Assuming that an object is in a state of free fall near the earth's surface, what is the formula for the speed in feet per second acquired by a falling body?
Answer: V = 32t (t is the time in seconds).

32) How long will it take for an object dropped from a height of 100 feet to reach the ground?
Answer: 2.5 seconds.

33) Which English poet wrote a famous ode after reviewing the ruins of an abbey? This abbey was named Tintern.
Answer: William Wordsworth.

34) Which 18th century satire by which person proposes an unusual solution for the food shortage resulting from the Irish potato famine?
Answer: *A Modest Proposal* by Jonathan Swift.

35) Identify the Attorney General of the Reagan administration who resigned when faced with charges of impropriety in 1988.
Answer: Edwin Meese.

36) Which New York Representative was denied his seat in the House of Representatives in 1967 on charges that he had misused government funds?
Answer: Adam Clayton Powell.

37) Which of the 3 influential styles of Greek columns was the simplest?
Answer: Doric.

38) The artistic works on the Acropolis in Athens were created under the direction of which sculptor, considered the greatest of the ancient Greek sculptors?
Answer: Phidias.

39) Which European city suffered a great fire in September 1666?
Answer: London.

40) Identify the 2 countries that signed an accord on September 17, 1978, at Camp David, Maryland, after President Jimmy Carter oversaw the negotiations.

Answer: Israel and Egypt (called the Camp David Accords; Israel and Egypt signed a peace treaty March 26, 1979).

41) What is the base 2 representation of the number 6?
Answer: 110.

42) Give the word for one billion characters of information in the field of computers.
Answer: Gigabyte.

43) Who was the first President to walk to his inauguration, doing so on March 4, 1801?
Answer: Thomas Jefferson.

44) Identify the British officer hanged as a spy on October 2, 1780. He and Benedict Arnold had planned to capture the vital American fort at West Point.
Answer: Major John André.

45) What is the capital of Vermont?
Answer: Montpelier.

46) Which U.S. President called his estate Montpelier?
Answer: James Madison.

47) What is the value of negative 2 to the 4th power?
Answer: 16.

48) If the measure of one of 2 congruent angles of an isosceles triangle is 20 degrees, what is the degree measure of the 3rd angle?
Answer: 140.

49) Of what nationality was chemist Alfred Bernhard Nobel, the inventor of dynamite and the originator of the Nobel Prizes?
Answer: Swedish.

50) Economics is one of the 6 Nobel Prizes. Name 3 of the other 5 Prizes.
Answer: Physics, chemistry, physiology or medicine, literature, and peace.

51) How many stars are in our solar system?
Answer: One (the sun).

52) Name the Greek astronomer who in the 100s B.C. drew up the first catalog of stars, showing their brightness and position.
Answer: Hipparchus.

53) Which Frenchman wrote *The Three Musketeers*?
Answer: Alexandre Dumas (père; he wrote it with Auguste Maquet).

54) Identify 2 of the Three Musketeers of Alexandre Dumas, père.
Answer: Athos, Porthos, and Aramis.

55) Name the U.S. Supreme Court justice who served the longest term at 36 years.
Answer: William O. Douglas.

56) Which act provided for the enforcing of national prohibition of the use of intoxicating liquors?
Answer: Volstead Act.

57) The stock prices of 500 companies are represented in the major S&P indexes, statistics which measure changes in American stock market prices. For what do the letters S&P stand?
Answer: Standard & Poor.

58) In the stock market parlance, which word is used to identify "the reversal of the trend of stock prices, especially temporarily, after a sharp decline or sharp rise in the trading sessions"?
Answer: Correction.

59) Which country brought back the Panchen Lama to share nominal political power and spiritual rule in Tibet?
Answer: China.

60) Name the supreme ruler of Tibet until Chinese Communists invaded his country in 1950. This ruler fled into exile in India in 1959.
Answer: Dalai Lama.

61) Which term used in meteorology designates "a line on a weather map connecting points having the same average temperature"?
Answer: Isotherm.

62) Which term used in meteorology designates "a line on a weather map connecting points having the same average barometric pressure"?
Answer: Isobar.

63) Identify the designer and sculptor of the Statue of Liberty.
Answer: Frédéric Auguste Bartholdi.

64) Give the complete English name of the Statue of Liberty.
Answer: Liberty Enlightening the World.

65) In which U.S. state did the first sanctuary for wild horses open up at Hell's Canyon near Hot Springs in the Black Hills in 1988?
Answer: South Dakota.

66) In which U.S. state are Fort Larned, Fort Riley, and Fort Leavenworth?
Answer: Kansas.

67) If there are 16 1/2 feet in one rod, how many feet are there in 6 rods?
Answer: 99.

68) If the sum of the lengths of the edges of a cube is 120 inches, what is the area of one face of the cube?
Answer: 100 square inches.

69) In which Scandinavian city is the Nobel Peace Prize presented?
Answer: Oslo (Norway).

70) Identify the city and country in which the other 5 Nobel Prizes are presented.
Answer: Stockholm, Sweden.

71) James Lind, a Scottish physician, found that adding lemon juice or orange juice to the diet of sailors on a very long sea voyage cured and prevented which disease?
Answer: Scurvy.

72) Of the Black Death, smallpox, cholera, and influenza, which one is spread through contaminated food or water?
Answer: Cholera.

73) In which Shakespearean play do the following characters appear: Desdemona, Iago, and Cassio?
Answer: *Othello.*

74) In which Shakespearean play do the following characters appear: Earl of Gloucester, Edgar, and Edmund?
Answer: *King Lear.*

75) How often according to the Constitution does Congress use a census count to reapportion the House of Representatives?
Answer: **Every 10 years.**

76) Who presides over the Senate in the absence of the Vice President?
Answer: **The President *pro tempore*.**

77) Who is the Roman equivalent of the Greek Zeus?
Answer: **Jupiter (also called Jove).**

78) Identify the animal that is the chief symbol of Athena, the Greek goddess of wisdom.
Answer: **Owl.**

79) Identify the "Congress" held in 1814-1815 that divided up Napoleon's empire after the Napoleonic Wars.
Answer: **Congress of Vienna.**

80) Identify the "Congress" held in 1856 that settled the problems that were produced by the Crimean War.
Answer: **Congress of Paris.**

81) Which U.S. President coined the phrase "United Nations" during Winston Churchill's visit to Washington in 1941?
Answer: **Franklin D. Roosevelt (In his memoirs, Churchill gives the credit to Roosevelt).**

82) Give the meaning of the acronym UNICEF.
Answer: **United Nations Children's Fund (originally United Nations International Children's Emergency Fund).**

83) Identify the U.S. President who issued the preliminary Emancipation Proclamation on September 22, 1862.
Answer: **Abraham Lincoln.**

84) Which captain uttered which famous words on September 23, 1779, in response to a request for surrender issued by the captain of the H.M.S. *Serapis*?
Answer: John Paul Jones said, "Sir, I have not yet begun to fight."

85) Which U.S. city had most of its buildings burned in 1864? This city became the state capital in 1868, and it is the home of the High Museum of Art, the Carter Library, and the Martin Luther King, Jr., tomb.
Answer: Atlanta (Georgia).

86) Name 4 of the 5 U.S. states bordering the Gulf of Mexico.
Answer: Texas, Louisiana, Mississippi, Alabama, and Florida.

87) If a circle is inscribed about a square of diagonal 40, what is the length of the radius of the circle?
Answer: 20.

88) What is the length of the hypotenuse of a right triangle if the other sides are of length 6 and 8?
Answer: 10.

89) In which country is Lillehammer, the city that was awarded the 1994 Winter Olympic Games?
Answer: Norway.

90) Identify the American swimmer who won 7 medals in the 1988 Summer Olympics.
Answer: Matt Biondi (5 gold, 1 silver, and 1 bronze).

91) Give the word used to designate the calm, low-pressure center of a hurricane around which winds of high velocity move.
Answer: Eye.

92) What number designates a catastrophic hurricane, the highest possible and one assigned to Hurricane Gilbert in 1988?
Answer: (Category) 5.

93) Which word completes the lines of the poem "The New Colossus" about the Statue of Liberty: "A mighty woman with a torch,

whose flame / Is the imprisoned lightning, and her name / Mother of ________"?
Answer: "Exiles."

94) Which author wrote the poem "The New Colossus," a poem inscribed on a bronze placard in the pedestal of the Statue of Liberty?
Answer: Emma Lazarus.

95) Which amendment, added to the U.S. Constitution in 1967, provides for the removal of the President if the Vice President and a majority of the cabinet declare him "unable to discharge the powers and duties of his office"?
Answer: 25th Amendment.

96) Who shot and wounded President Reagan and James Brady on March 30, 1981?
Answer: John Hinckley.

97) Of which unique and august French body established to maintain good taste in French language and style did Marguerite Yourcenar become the first woman member in 1981?
Answer: Académie Française (or French Academy).

98) Which Cardinal established the French Academy in 1635?
Answer: Cardinal Richelieu.

99) In which country is the period from 1867 to 1912 known as the Meiji Period? *Meiji* means *enlightened rule*, a term which Emperor Mutsuhito adopted as his title.
Answer: Japan.

100) In which country is Babi Yar? Many gather in this ravine to commemorate the Nazi massacre of Jews that occurred there on September 28-29, 1941, during WWII.
Answer: Soviet Union (near Kiev).

CHAPTER TWENTY

1) Complete the epitaph on the tombstone of Edgar Allan Poe,
   "Quoth the __________ nevermore."
   Answer: "Raven."

2) Identify the man whose diary raised new doubts in 1988 about
   his claim that on April 6, 1909, he became the first man to reach
   the North Pole.
   Answer: Robert Peary.

3) Identify the American organization named for a Baptist missionary and WWII U.S. Air Force officer shot by Chinese Communists in 1945.
   Answer: John Birch Society.

4) Identify the much-maligned organization Roger Baldwin founded
   in 1920 to combat the deportation of aliens as ordered by
   Attorney General A. Mitchell Palmer.
   Answer: American Civil Liberties Union.

5) Identify the largest mountain system of North America.
   Answer: Rocky Mountains.

6) Identify the mountains in northeastern New York whose name
   is derived from the Indian word for "bark (tree) eaters." Mt.
   Marcy is their highest point and the highest in the state.
   Answer: Adirondack Mountains.

7) The front of the Parthenon in Athens is shaped like a special
   rectangle, the measure of whose sides is always in the ratio of
   about 1 to 1.618. What kind of "colorful" rectangle is it?
   Answer: Golden.

8) If you bisect an angle of 180 degrees into 2 congruent angles and
   then divide both of those angles into 4 congruent angles, how

many degrees will be in an angle complementary to one of the small angles?
Answer: 67 1/2 degrees.

9) Give the nationality of Kristin Otto at the time this swimmer won 6 gold medals at the 1988 Summer Olympic Games.
Answer: East German.

10) Which athlete from which country won the 100-meter dash in the 1988 Olympics with the fastest time in history at 9.79 seconds before he was stripped of his medal for drug abuse?
Answer: Ben Johnson from Canada (Carl Lewis was awarded the medal).

11) Which Frenchman discovered natural radioactivity in 1896?
Answer: Antoine Henri Becquerel.

12) Identify the isotopes of hydrogen with twice and three times the mass of ordinary hydrogen.
Answer: Deuterium (or heavy hydrogen) and tritium.

13) Which American writer was born Truman Streckfus Persons? He wrote *In Cold Blood* and *Answered Prayers*.
Answer: Truman Capote.

14) Identify the character whose name completes the title of T.S. Eliot's poem, *The Love Song of J. Alfred* __________.
Answer: *Prufrock*.

15) Although Washington, D.C., has a mayor and city council, which body governs this district?
Answer: Congress.

16) Give 2 of the 3 requirements to become a member of the U.S. Senate.
Answer: 30 years of age, a citizen of the U.S. for 9 years, and a resident of the state which elects him.

17) Give the meaning of the phrase *pro bono* or *pro bono publico* that identifies the work performed by some law firms or by some lawyers.
Answer: "Done without charge" or "for the public good."

18) In which field would one find Grimm's Law, Verner's Law, and Grassmann's Law? In this field, Noam Chomsky contributed his Generative Theory in the 1950s.
Answer: Language, linguistics, or phonetics and philology.

19) Identify the city in western Thrace near the Aegean coast that King Philip II of Macedonia founded in 357 B.C.
Answer: Philippi.

20) Identify the 2 men who defeated Brutus and Cassius Longius at the Battle of Philippi in 42 B.C.
Answer: Mark Antony and Octavian (later Augustus).

21) On the banks of which New York river is the United Nations building located?
Answer: East River.

22) Which wealthy American gave $8 1/2 million to buy 18 acres of land for the United Nations' building?
Answer: John D. Rockefeller, Jr.

23) Which British explorer's ships were named the *Endeavour*, the *Resolution*, the *Adventure*, and the *Discovery*?
Answer: James Cook.

24) Identify the black who was the only American to accompany Robert E. Peary when the explorer allegedly reached the North Pole.
Answer: Matthew Henson.

25) In which country did Hurricane Gilbert ravage the Yucatan Peninsula in 1988?
Answer: Mexico.

26) Identify the British dependency in the Caribbean Sea whose capital and largest city is Georgetown.
Answer: Cayman Islands.

27) How many tons is 450,000 pounds?
Answer: 225.

28) If the log of 2.0 is 0.301, what will be the log of 8.0?
Answer: 0.903.

29) Identify the American who in the 1988 Olympics won a gold medal in the heptathlon and set a new world record in the process.
Answer: Jackie Joyner-Kersee.

30) Name 3 of the events in the Olympic heptathlon.
Answer: 100-meter hurdles, shot-put, high jump, 200-meter run, long jump, javelin, and 800-meter run.

31) Which word means "the act of changing into stone"? In this process dissolved minerals are carried by groundwater into the empty cells of the decaying wood until the structure has become solid stone.
Answer: Petrifaction (accept petrification).

32) In which desert in which state is the Petrified Forest National Park?
Answer: Painted Desert in Arizona.

33) Which U.S. author popularized local-color stories about the West with his mining camp tales?
Answer: Bret Harte.

34) Which work by which Roman writer features Troy and the story of the Trojan Horse?
Answer: *Aeneid* by Virgil.

35) Identify the term used in the U.S. Congress to designate a method of cutting off debate to force a vote on a particular question.
Answer: Cloture.

36) By law, Congress cannot suspend the legal order that protects people from being jailed illegally on weak evidence or none at all except during an invasion or rebellion. Give the Latin used to name this right.
Answer: Writ of habeas corpus.

37) In his *Confessions* he wrote, "Give me chastity and continence, but not just now." Name this 4th-5th century North African

theologian and bishop who was one of the most influential leaders of the early Christian Church.
Answer: St. Augustine.

38) Name the Christian humanist of the Renaissance, known as the "Scholar of Europe," who wrote *In Praise of Folly* in 1509.
Answer: Desiderius Erasmus.

39) Name the U.S. President at the signing of the U.N. Charter on June 26, 1945, when Secretary of State Edward R. Stettinius signed for the United States.
Answer: Harry S Truman.

40) In which European city did the first session of the U.N. General Assembly open in early 1946?
Answer: London.

41) What is the name given to a line containing a diameter of a circle?
Answer: Secant.

42) What is the word used to describe 2 circles that lie in the same plane and have exactly one point in common?
Answer: Tangent.

43) Which U.S. President's Farewell Address was published on September 19, 1796?
Answer: George Washington's.

44) Name the schoolteacher the British hanged as a spy whose famous last words may have been inspired by Joseph Addison's "What a pity is it / That we can die but once to serve our country!"
Answer: Nathan Hale.

45) Which Central American country is the largest in area with 50,200 square miles? It is located between Costa Rica and Honduras.
Answer: Nicaragua.

46) Which geyser complex in which U.S. national park was threatened by raging forest fires that destroyed several surrounding buildings in 1988?
Answer: Old Faithful Geyser in Yellowstone National Park.

47) How many square yards are there in a rectangular floor that is 3 feet by 6 feet?
Answer: 2 square yards.

48) If oranges are twice as expensive as apples, and apples sell at 2 pounds for a dollar, how much does a pound of oranges cost?
Answer: $1.00.

49) In which U.S. state is Edwards Air Force Base?
Answer: California.

50) In which city in which state is the Marshall Space Flight Center?
Answer: Huntsville, Alabama.

51) What is usually measured as the height in inches to which the atmosphere will force a column of mercury in an evacuated tube?
Answer: Barometric pressure.

52) Which word means "the process for the sorting of and allocation of first-aid treatment to victims, as of a battle or disaster, on the basis of urgency, to maximize the number of survivors"?
Answer: Triage.

53) Who is the American author of the play *The Glass Menagerie*?
Answer: Tennessee Williams.

54) In which city is the play *The Glass Menagerie* set?
Answer: St. Louis.

55) Congress is given the power to establish uniform taxes. Give the word for "taxes on goods coming into the U.S."
Answer: Duties.

56) Give the word for "taxes on the manufacture, sale, or use of goods made within the country."
Answer: Excise taxes.

57) Give the English translation of the Latin phrase *Ars gratia artis*.
Answer: "Art for art's sake."

58) Give the English translation of the Latin phrase *Ars longa, vita brevis*.
Answer: "Art is long, (but) life is short."

59) Which area of Czechoslovakia was ceded to Germany in 1938 in hopes of averting war and having "peace with honor"? Six months later when Germany marched into Prague, any pretense of peace and honor was ended.
Answer: Sudetenland.

60) Chamberlain of Britain and Hitler of Germany signed the Munich Pact in 1938. Identify the leaders of Italy and France who also signed.
Answer: Mussolini (Italy) and Daladier (France).

61) Which of the following adjectives designates "of or having to do with meteorological data from simultaneous observations at many points": *kinetic, synoptic, anabatic,* or *gradient*?
Answer: Synoptic.

62) Which of the following terms designates "wisps of rain or snow falling from a cloud that dissipate before they reach the ground": *virga, allobar, vibrissa,* or *varix*?
Answer: Virga.

63) Which U.S. President was elected to the Senate after he survived an impeachment trial?
Answer: Andrew Johnson.

64) Name the first 2 U.S. Presidents to serve just one term each.
Answer: John Adams and John Quincy Adams.

65) In which country did the U.S. abandon the strategic naval base at Cam Ranh Bay?
Answer: Vietnam.

66) Name the 2 largest U.S. military installations outside the U.S. They are both located in the Philippines.
Answer: Subic Bay Naval Base and Clark Air Base.

67) What is the sum of the prime factors of 21?
Answer: 10.

68) If peanuts sell for $4.00 a pound, how much will 12 ounces sell for?
Answer: $3.00.

69) The U.S. signed with 11 countries to build a $23 billion space station by 1996. Name this station that will be built in orbit through 22 shuttle flights over 3 years.
Answer: *Freedom.*

70) In which city in which state is the Johnson Space Flight Center?
Answer: Houston, Texas.

71) What family of elements has the least reactive stable atoms?
Answer: Noble gases or inert gases.

72) Name the English astronomer and mathematician who was instrumental in the publishing of Sir Isaac Newton's major work on gravitation, *Principia Mathematica*. He encouraged and paid for the publication of this masterpiece.
Answer: Edmond Halley.

73) Which work by Charles Dickens is admittedly autobiographical? This novel's small boy is sent by his cruel stepfather to Mr. Creakle's school.
Answer: *David Copperfield.*

74) In *The Merchant of Venice*, what does Antonio promise to give Shylock if he is unable to repay the loan in three months?
Answer: A pound of flesh.

75) Give the word for "an official document that gives an inventor exclusive right to his invention."
Answer: Patent.

76) Give the word for "the exclusive right to publish a literary work."
Answer: Copyright.

77) NYSE is the largest U.S. stock exchange. What is the meaning of the initials NYSE?
Answer: New York Stock Exchange.

78) NYSE is the largest U.S. stock exchange and AMEX is the second largest. Give the meaning of the initials AMEX.
Answer: American Stock Exchange.

79) Identify 2 of the 3 members of the defense agreement known as the Triple Alliance, which lasted from 1882 until WWI (1915).
Answer: Austria-Hungary, Germany, and Italy.

80) Identify 2 of the 3 countries that formed the Triple Entente, an alignment that resulted from a series of bilateral agreements among them between 1894 and 1907.
Answer: Great Britain, France, and Russia.

81) What is the full name of CORE, the civil rights organization founded in 1942 in Chicago?
Answer: Congress of Racial Equality.

82) Who helped to establish CORE and served as its national director until 1966?
Answer: James Farmer.

83) Which Presidential candidate committed a gaffe in 1976 by saying that Poland was no longer under Soviet domination?
Answer: Gerald Ford (while debating Jimmy Carter).

84) President Reagan campaigned for George Bush in 1988. Name the only 2 Presidents in this century who had the opportunity to campaign for their Vice President while still in office but declined to do so. Both Vice Presidents lost their presidential races.
Answer: Dwight Eisenhower (for Richard Nixon) and Lyndon Johnson (for Hubert Humphrey).

85) Name the 2 countries on the island of Hispaniola in the Caribbean Sea.
Answer: Haiti and the Dominican Republic.

86) Name the capitals of both Haiti and the Dominican Republic.
Answer: Port-au-Prince (Haiti) and Santo Domingo (Dominican Republic).

87) What mathematical term is used to describe a special correspondence that assigns to each member of one set exactly one value from another set?
Answer: Function.

88) What is the principal square root of 576?
Answer: 24.

89) Give the term referring to the winning of all 4 major tennis titles.
Answer: Grand Slam (the term, taken from the game of bridge, refers to the winning of all 13 tricks).

90) Which teenager from which country in 1988 became the 5th tennis player to win the Grand Slam in a calendar year?
Answer: Steffi Graf from West Germany.

91) Which muscle on the back of the arm has 3 points or 3 heads?
Answer: Triceps.

92) To which scientific class do all mosses belong?
Answer: Musci.

93) Which American author's autobiographical work, *A Moveable Feast*, is based on notebooks he kept in Paris during the 1920s?
Answer: Ernest Hemingway.

94) What is the name of the kingdom of Prince Rupert in *The Prisoner of Zenda*?
Answer: Ruritania.

95) In which daily account are the proceedings of both the U.S. Senate and the House of Representatives published?
Answer: Congressional Record.

96) What is the family name of 5 English printers who published reports of Parliament's sessions from 1774 to 1889? This name today identifies the official printed report of the proceedings in Parliament.
Answer: Hansard.

97) Give the surname shared by 3 noted anthropologists whose first names are Louis (S.B.), Mary (D.), and Richard (E.F.).
Answer: Leakey.

98) In which gorge in which African country did Louis and Mary Leakey find and name the species *Homo habilis*, identifying it as the earliest member in the genus of human beings?
Answer: Olduvai Gorge in Tanzania.

99) Identify the African country where King Sobhuza died in 1982 after a reign of 82 years. His son, Prince Makhosetive, took the throne in 1986 and became known as King Mswati III. This country's capital is Mbabane.
Answer: Swaziland.

100) The Persians destroyed most buildings on the Acropolis of Athens in 480 B.C. Name the great statesman under whose leadership the Athenians began to rebuild the site in 447 B.C.
Answer: **Pericles.**

2001) Which 1968 work by which author is subtitled *A Space Odyssey*?
Answer: *2001* **by Arthur C. Clarke.**